NAME, PLACE, MAGIC!

Shweta Ganesh Kumar is an award-winning writer, blogger, and senior developmental editor. She is the author of five children's books including *Leela's Special Day*, *The Tiffin Gang*, *At Home*, and *What House Shall I Build Today?*. Her books have been featured at the New York Public Library's World Literature Festival and the Children's Museum of Manhattan's India Week.

Shweta hosts the podcast *Storytelling with Shweta* on Spotify and lives in New York City with her husband, two children, and their dog.

NAME, PLACE, MAGIC!

Stories of How Indian States Got Their Names

SHWETA GANESH KUMAR

Inside Illustrations by Vibha Surya

hachette
INDIA

First published in paperback in 2025 by Hachette India
(Registered name: Hachette Book Publishing India Pvt. Ltd)
An Hachette UK company
www.hachetteindia.com

1

ISBN 978-93-5731-291-2

Hachette Book Publishing India Pvt. Ltd
4th & 5th Floors, Corporate Centre
Plot No. 94, Sector 44, Gurugram – 122003, India

Typeset by Manmohan Kumar, Delhi

Printed and bound in India
by Manipal Technologies Limited

FSC www.fsc.org MIX Paper | Supporting responsible forestry FSC™ C043100

CONTENTS

INTRODUCTION

Legends and tales have been a part of our history for a very, very long time. You see, long before our country came to be known for its vibrant cities, stunning landscapes, and delicious food, India was a land made up of numerous kingdoms and tribes. The places that we now know as the twenty-eight states of the country were once different territories or regions that were homes to various tribes. The people from these regions had stories about how their lands were formed and how the land got its name. Some of these stories had gods and goddesses, others had fierce warriors. Some had extraordinary people who meditated for thousands of years, and others had rivers and mountains that transformed into people. Some of these stories came from books that were written hundreds of years ago, while others were passed down through stories told by ancestors. It is important to remember that these tales are myths and legends which are not the same as historical facts. As stories are told again and again, people sometimes add new parts or forget others. That's how myths and legends grow and change over time. This book brings together exciting stories from every state in India, telling tales that began long, long ago.

And how did these stories spread? By being told. Have you ever played the game called 'Telephone'? It's when you think of a word and whisper it in your friend's ear, and they whisper it in the next friend's ear till the word that the last person says out loud is something completely different. In the same way, the stories about these Indian states have passed through so many ears and mouths that there are many different versions of them. So, as you read a story in this book, you might feel like you have heard this story before or a different version of it or never heard this story at all. But that's okay. All readers are welcome to dive into this version of the legends behind the twenty-eight Indian states. Of course, India is not just about the states, we also have eight Union Territories with rather unique names and reasons why they are named that way. Dive into these stories that will take us on a journey across the land that is now known as India.

1

ANDHRA PRADESH

The Land of the Andhra People

Many, many years ago, before the people of Andhra were known as Andhras, there lived a sage named Vishwamitra. Sage Vishwamitra was not just another holy man, but one of the most respected of the seven Brahmarishis of olden times. The Brahmarishis were very important people, the highest class of sages. As expected, Sage Vishwamitra was a serious man with bushy eyebrows, a long grey beard, and hair flecked with black and white, tied up in a bun on the top of his head. He was supposed to be so knowledgeable that every king and queen wanted him to be their royal priest. He was very good at religious ceremonies and made sure that every god and goddess was nicely honoured. The one flaw he had, though, was his temper. People who were close to him used to say that his anger lived on the tip of his nose, which was just an interesting way of saying that Sage Vishwamitra would get angry quite easily.

This made things quite hard for his children, and he had a lot of them. Sage Vishwamitra lived on earth for a very long time, and over the course of those years he had one hundred children. You would think this was enough, but Sage Vishwamitra decided he would like to add one more to his brood of children. The boy he chose was Shunahshepa, the middle son of his sister.

You might be wondering why Sage Vishwamitra wanted to adopt Shunahshepa, his nephew, as one of his sons. Shunahshepa had been given away by his parents to the king of their land. The king had taken the boy to a religious ceremony, or a puja, over which Sage Vishwamitra had presided. Now that the puja was over and the king had gotten all that he needed, he did not want the boy anymore. And sadly, neither did the boy's parents. However, Sage Vishwamitra had seen Shunahshepa's usefulness during the puja. Shunahshepa had been able to call on the gods, and the gods had given him many boons as well. Sage Vishwamitra knew that he would be able to train Shunahshepa and hone his skills, so he decided to adopt the boy.

Sage Vishwamitra called all hundred of his sons to meet Shunahshepa. Fifty of his sons were older than

Shunahshepa, and fifty of them were younger. He instructed them all to bow to Shunahshepa and then he told them that Shunahshepa would be their new older brother – the eldest, in fact. Sage Vishwamitra's sons were shocked. In the times that they lived in, an elder brother in the family was almost as powerful as the parents of the family. How could their father just bring in a cousin they had not even met since childhood and make him the second most important person in their family? What did their father mean by this act? For years, they had lived in his holy hermitage, his ashram, and studied under him. They had done everything he had told them to and hoped that one day they would be powerful sages with hermitages of their own. Now, their father had brought in an outsider to inherit his position as a respected sage!

The fifty sons who were younger than Shunahshepa reluctantly agreed to accept Sage Vishwamitra's decision. They needed the guidance of someone older, and having one more older brother did not really make a difference to them when they already had so many older than them. They bowed to Shunahshepa and quietly walked over to Sage Vishwamitra's side. The great sage was delighted, and now he looked at his fifty oldest children, who continued to remain silent.

His children had always obeyed him. He was proud of how intelligent, compassionate and loving they were. They had always taken care of their younger brothers and other responsibilities when Sage Vishwamitra was in other lands for work. So now, what was taking them so long to agree?

Sage Vishwamitra raised a bushy eyebrow at the eldest. He waited for him to walk over with his brothers, indicating that he, too, agreed with his father's decision. However, to the sage's shock, his eldest son shook his head. He stepped forward, crossed his arms in front of him and told Sage Vishwamitra that he did not accept his decision. The sage was immediately enraged; he scrunched up his forehead and narrowed his eyes.

'How dare you question my decision?' the sage thundered at them. 'I am telling you again that I have decided to adopt Shunahshepa as my eldest son. And you will abide by my decision. You must walk over and stand here beside me to show your agreement,' Sage Vishwamitra yelled.

But the sage's sons had inherited his pride. The fifty of them stood strong, and refused.

'If that is the case, then I hereby banish you to the southern part of the land. You will go far away from here and live in the south, where you will be known as Andhras, and I will never see you ever again.'

The sons of Vishwamitra were taken aback by their father's decision. But they never once thought of defying their father. He meant the world to them, even if they disagreed with him. So they bowed to their father, bid farewell to their younger brothers, and left

on their long journey down south. They went to the River Ganga where they used to take their bath every morning and took a last dip before they said goodbye to the land they had always called their home. Then, the brothers, known as Andhras, started their travel. They walked through jungles and crossed mountains. They waded through rivers and passed through other large kingdoms till they finally reached the banks of a river so wide and fast that it reminded them of their own River Ganga.

'This will be our Dakshin Ganga. This will be the Ganga of the South,' the eldest of the brothers said as he left his belongings on the banks of the river and stepped into the crystal clear waters. His brothers agreed. They soon settled down in the land that the river flowed through. As years passed, the land came to be known as the Land of the Andhras – a land filled with people who were known for their love of learning, their thick hair, and their sweet language. The river flowing through their land was later called River Godavari, but it is still also known as the Ganga of the South. And the land itself was named Andhra Pradesh.

KNOW YOUR STATES

- Andhra Pradesh is sometimes called the 'Kohinoor of India' because the famous Koh-i-Noor diamond is believed to have come from a mine in Guntur, a place in Andhra Pradesh.
- The capital of Andhra Pradesh is Amaravati. Amaravati literally means 'the place where immortals live.'
- Pingali Venkayya, the person who designed the Indian national flag, was from Andhra Pradesh. He was also a freedom fighter. The first version of the flag had only red and green stripes. Later, Mahatma Gandhi suggested adding a white stripe in the middle to represent peace and include all communities.
- The official language of Andhra Pradesh is Telugu.
- Kuchipudi is a famous classical dance form from Andhra Pradesh.
- Andhra Pradesh is one of India's top mango-producing states – yum!
- Dharmavaram is a city in Andhra Pradesh that is famous for its beautiful silk saris. These saris are handwoven using pure mulberry silk.

2

ARUNACHAL PRADESH

The Land of Dawn-Lit Mountains

Once upon a time, high up in the tall mountains that lie in the north-east of the country that we now know as India, there lived a boy called Nyethri. Nyethri belonged to a tribe called the Monpa, who had lived in the mountains for as long as anyone could remember. Nyethri had seen his people weave, make baskets, and carve wood for as long as he could remember. His mother and father had told him that he, too, would have to choose one of these crafts to work with as he grew up. But Nyethri had a different dream.

When he saw the tall mountains touching the sky, all Nyethri wanted to do was climb them and see what was at the very top. There was one mountain in particular that the adventurous boy could not wait to climb – the Sacred Mountain that stood tall in the heart of their land. Nyethri's grandmother had told him stories of how the mountain held the secrets to the beginning of time.

'Look at the top, Nyethri. Our gods and goddesses live on the very top of that mountain,' she would say pointing to the peak of the Sacred Mountain, which was so high up that it seemed to touch the clouds.

Nyethri yearned to climb up to the top of the Sacred Mountain. Never mind that others thought it would be too challenging or that it might disturb the gods and goddesses, Nyethri could not wait for the day that he could start the climb. Day after day, he sat at the foot of the mountain, trying to figure out how he would get to the top. Finally, on the day he turned sixteen, he felt like he was ready. He packed a little bundle with cheese, meat, rice, and butter tea in a bottle. He bid goodbye to his parents, hugged his little brother and sister, and asked his grandparents to bless him on his journey. With his entire family and village wishing him the best, Nyethri placed his first step on the Sacred Mountain.

It was an uphill climb. As Nyethri went further and further, the slopes became steeper and steeper. But Nyethri did not give up. Days passed, and he climbed on, stopping once in a while for some food and never thinking about giving up. After his food and drinks ran out, Nyethri paused to look down the path he had climbed, but all he could see was a sea of clouds. He was so high up that the air was thin, and it looked like he had stepped into the kingdom of the gods. Nyethri closed his eyes and felt all his tiredness wash away as if something divine had come near him. He felt a voice tell him that the summit was near. He opened his eyes and continued his climb.

Finally, Nyethri was at the summit, where a wonderful sight was waiting for him. As he placed his first step on the very peak of the mountain, the clouds parted to reveal gorgeous flowers and plants, crystal clear lakes that sparkled, and mystical creatures that looked like they were from a different realm. Standing calmly in the centre of it all was a goddess. Nyethri bowed down to her and immediately recognized that she was the goddess his grandmother called the Lhamo or the 'Guardian of the Sacred Mountain.' The Lhamo had long flowing hair and the brightest eyes that

Nyethri had ever seen. She smiled at him, and he felt calm inside. 'Come close, my child,' the Lhamo raised her palm and beckoned Nyethri over.

'I am impressed by you, child. You have come so far, and you have gone through so many obstacles to hear the story of your land's birth, and as a reward, I shall tell you the story of your land,' the Lhamo said to Nyethri.

Nyethri hurried over to her and sat cross-legged next to the goddess to hear her tale.

'In the beginning of time, there was nothing but two golden eggs that moved around each other. Round and round they went till they dashed into each other and broke into pieces. One piece was the sky, and the other was the earth. The sky wanted to embrace the earth, but it was so big that it could not. So, the earth decided to make herself smaller. She took a deep breath and curled herself into a smaller piece making mountains and hills rise up to touch the morning sky as she folded into herself. The overjoyed sky hugged her, and when

the earth and sky came together, all the animals, plants, gods, and goddesses were created. This Sacred Mountain was one of the first mountains to rise up and touch the sky when the earth and sky came together, so this is where the gods and goddesses live as they keep an eye on the rest of the world's creations. Now that you know this secret you, too, must help in keeping the earth and her creatures alive and well.'

Nyethri was grateful that his quest for finding wisdom on top of the Sacred Mountain had been successful. He thanked the Lhamo and made his way back down to his people where he told them the story of how their land was formed, why the mountains were so important, and how all wisdom existed at the top of the dawn-lit mountains. Like the Lhamo had taught him, he taught his people why the natural world had to be protected and how they were supposed to live in harmony with the rest of the world.

Nyethri's story continues to be passed on from generation to generation as a reminder of the sacred mountains in the land – a land that would one day be called Arunachal Pradesh, meaning 'land of the dawn-lit mountains'. The name comes from the Sanskrit words *aruna* meaning 'dawn' and *achal* meaning 'mountain', with *pradesh* meaning 'land'.

KNOW YOUR STATES

- Arunachal Pradesh is also called the land of the rising sun. This is also because the word *aruna* in Arunachal means 'Sun.' The state's name can also mean 'the land where the sun rises from behind the mountains.'
- The people of the Monpa tribe perform a traditional dance called the Aji Lhamu. They believe this dance helps them connect with their ancestors and brings them blessings from the gods.
- Itanagar is the capital of Arunachal Pradesh. Itanagar gets its name from the Ita Fort, or the 'Fort of Bricks,' situated in the heart of the city.
- Arunachal Pradesh is inhabited by twenty-six major tribes and over hundred sub-tribes.
- The famous Tawang Monastery in Arunachal Pradesh is the largest Buddhist monastery in India and the second largest in the world.
- The forests of Arunachal Pradesh are home to some very rare animals, like red pandas, clouded leopards and the hoolock gibbon – India's only ape.

3

ASSAM

The Land of the Ahom People

According to an ancient legend from the land now known as Assam, in the very beginning, there was nothing but the vast waters of the ocean. There were no lands or people. No plants or animals. No sound could be heard except the splashing of the waters of this ocean. There was neither the earth nor the heaven nor the sun nor the stars. But there was one being – the creator god called Pha Thu Ching, who was shapeless and voiceless and lay spread through this universe that was nothing but the ocean. It is hard to imagine what Pha Thu Ching looked like, he neither had a head nor legs. He did not have a mouth, but he did have eyes. Pha Thu Ching, being a god, knew that he would have to change his form and create other beings if he wanted to be celebrated and revered. So Pha Thu Ching opened his eyes one day and decided that it was time to create something he would like to look at. So he created the first deity called Khun Theu Kham. Khun Theu Kham, in turn, looked around and saw nothing to lean on, so he dived into the water and leaned on his back, and a lotus plant sprouted up from his navel. Next from his navel came a crab, then a tortoise, and then an eight-headed snake that encircled the tortoise and stretched out in eight directions.

Now, it was time to create the earth. The deity took a deep breath, and out sprung a white elephant with tusks carrying two mountains. One mountain was dropped in north and the other in south. Then, two pillars were placed on the mountains, and a giant rope was used to connect both pillars. This was followed by two spiders made of gold who fell down from the creator. The spiders created the earth and then quickly went spinning back and forth, back and forth, and wove an intricate web that they attached to the top of the pillars. The spiders then made the heavens in the shape of a throne. As soon as the heavens had taken shape, Pha Thu Ching created a goddess to be Khun Theu Khem's partner. Together, they created eggs that would later hatch to become many gods and goddesses living in the heavens.

Years passed, and the gods and goddesses got together and decided to have a religious ceremony, a puja, to create two brothers to send down to earth. First, an octagonal altar called a 'Deoghar' was constructed. Around it sat: Khao Kham, the god of water; Ai Leng Din, the god of earth; Jan Chai Hung, who was the Lord of the gods; Jasingpha, the goddess of wisdom; Mut Kum Tai Kum, the deity of the Sun and the Moon; and the most important of all, Lengdon, the ruler of the universe. Together, the gods and goddesses created two human beings – the brothers Khun Lung and Khun Lai, and sent them down to the earth. The deities gave them a box with a divine idol called Sumdeo, a sword called the mighty Hengdon, a pair of drums, and two roosters. The deities told them to rule their kingdom on earth as the gods and goddesses decided.

Khun Lung and Khun Lai took charge of their kingdom down on earth. They took care of their people and did religious rituals honouring the gods as they had been told to. As time passed, the two brothers wanted to have their own countries to rule, so Khun Lung moved away, and many years later, so did his descendant Sukhapha. Prince Sukhapha respected the hillside country where he had grown up. Still, the prince dreamt of ruling a land that he had established himself. He decided he would travel far away and make his way up the winding mountains that he could see from his kingdom. When he turned nineteen, Prince Sukhapha put together a team of nine thousand people, three hundred horses, and two elephants and embarked on his adventure to create his own kingdom. When he left, he brought with him the divine idol, a divine elephant, a divine chicken, the divine sword Hengdon, and the embroidered cloth that Khun Lung, his ancestor who had descended from the heavens, had worn.

It was a long and arduous journey, and Prince Sukhapha and his people stopped at various locations. They learnt the languages of the people they met on the way and discovered new and different ways of cultivation. Prince Sukhapha and his people crossed many, many rivers and were affected by the floods that were common in the rivers of this new land. Years passed, but Prince Sukhapha still had not decided where he wanted to build his capital. Meanwhile, his people continued to follow him wherever he went, no matter what challenges they had to overcome along the way.

Finally, thirteen years after Prince Sukhapha had left the kingdom that his heavenly ancestor had established, he founded his own kingdom, which was known as the first Ahom kingdom. The people who had followed him here were known as the Ahoms. Prince Sukhapha ended up being a great king, and he always remained in awe of the strength and perseverance of his people. Legend says that he often used to call them Asama, which meant 'the people who were undefeated and invincible.' As time passed, the land that was once known as the Ahom kingdom came to be known as the 'land of the invincible Ahoms or Asama' – the land known as Assam.

KNOW YOUR STATES

- Assam is famous for its tea! It has some of the biggest tea-growing areas in the world. Assam tea is known all over the globe for its strong and rich flavor. The city of Jorhat is home to the oldest and largest tea research center in the world, called the Tocklai Tea Research Institute. It was started in 1911.
- The capital of Assam is Dispur.
- The largest city in Assam is Guwahati. The old name of the city was Pragjyotishpur, which means 'the light of the east.'
- Assam has its own state anthem, which was adopted in 1927. It is called 'O Mur Apunar Dex', which means 'O My Dearest Country' in Assamese.
- Assam is home to the one-horned rhinoceros. They can be seen in the Kaziranga National Park.
- Bihu is a series of harvest festivals celebrated in Assam that honor nature, new beginnings, and thankfulness for a good harvest.
- The traditional clothing of the women of Assam is a two-piece sari-like garment called the Mekhela Chador. The men wear a dhoti and gamosa.

4

BIHAR

The Land of the Ancient Buddhist Monasteries

Once upon a time, in a small kingdom nestled in the foothills of the Himalayas, a king was visited by a famous astrologer who told people's fortune by studying at the stars. The astrologer then prophesied this about the king's newborn son:

'O King, this son of yours will either grow up to be a great king or a holy man.'

The king was upset by the prophecy. He certainly did not want his child to become a holy man. So, he decided to raise him in utmost luxury within the walls of the palace and never let him leave the palace grounds. The child was named Siddhartha Gautama, and for twenty-nine years he was raised without ever seeing pain, sadness, or knowing anything about human suffering.

As he grew up, Siddhartha started feeling restless. He was married now, and he had a child, but he felt like there was more to life. He told his father that as he was to be the king of these lands, he wanted to see more of the kingdom. Reluctantly, the king agreed and sent him off on a chariot to see the parts of the kingdom that were better off than others. The chariot rolled out through the palace gates, and for the first time, Siddhartha Gautama feasted his eyes on the world outside. After a while, he saw an old man hobbling away on the other side of the road while leaning on a big, wooden stick.

'Why is he doing that?' Siddhartha asked the charioteer.

'He is very old, my Prince. Sometimes, in old age, we have to use things like sticks to support ourselves while walking. We all get old,' the charioteer replied.

They kept moving, and in a short while, the prince saw a man sitting by the road, looking tired and coughing loudly with his head in his hands.

'Why is he doing that?' Siddhartha asked the charioteer.

'He is sick, O Prince. His illness has left him weary. We all get sick,' the charioteer replied.

Siddhartha remained silent and kept his gaze on the outside world. After some time, they saw a crowd of people carrying a dead man. Men and women were crying and following the procession.

'Why are they crying? What is all this about?' Siddhartha asked the charioteer.

'The man being carried is dead, my Prince. The people following him are mourning his passing. Death comes to us all,' the charioteer replied.

That night, back in the palace, Siddhartha realized that he could not stop thinking of all the suffering he had seen. He knew that he could not do anything to take away people's suffering if he continued to stay in his palace in great luxury. Still, maybe he could find a solution outside of these palace gates. Siddhartha decided to leave behind his family and his life as a prince to go and search for meaning in life. He left behind his wife, Yashodhara, and his son, Rahula, and decided to become a holy monk. For six years, Siddhartha travelled from place to place in search of a holy teacher who could guide him and instruct him on the path to salvation. Yet, he never found peace or enlightenment.

By now, Siddhartha had travelled so far away from his kingdom that he had reached the banks of a river called Niranjana. There, he decided to throw himself into the harshest of meditations by denying himself food and water until he gained all the spiritual knowledge he wanted. Siddhartha sat himself down by the river and started meditating, but apart from getting frail and tired, he was nowhere near the goals he wanted to achieve.

One day, just as he was about to give up from exhaustion, he was approached by a woman holding a bowl of milk-rice. This was Sujata, who had been passing by with offerings for her favourite deity in a nearby temple. As she had walked past, she had seen the terribly thin and exhausted Siddhartha and decided that he needed the milk-rice more than the god did.

Siddhartha accepted the milk-rice with gratitude. He ate every last morsel and felt himself nourished not just by the food but also by the compassion Sujata had shown him. Siddhartha felt as if that day was the day he would receive the knowledge that would help him help others deal with their suffering. He sat down again, this time under a giant fig tree, and meditated. When he opened his eyes, he shone with the golden glow of wisdom. He understood it all now and had become Buddha, the enlightened one. The fig tree that he meditated under came to be known as the Bodhi tree, which translates to 'tree of enlightenment.'

Once Siddhartha Gautama became the Buddha, he came up with the Middle Way, which consisted of eight principles that people could follow to live a better life. The Buddha, as he was known, henceforth started preaching sermons. His teachings became famous, and hundreds and hundreds of people began gathering to hear his life lessons. Not just ordinary men but kings and nobility, too, started following the Buddha's eight-fold path.

The Bodhi tree under which the Buddha had gained enlightenment was part of the ancient kingdom of Magadha. The king of Magadha, Bimbisara, also welcomed the Buddha and his teachings with open arms. He invited the Buddha to establish monasteries of Buddhist monks in his kingdom. These monasteries were called *vihara*s. The land where the Buddha gained enlightenment and established these viharas was eventually called 'Vihara' by all the people who flocked there to become Buddhists themselves. As time passed, the land of these ancient Buddhist monasteries became known as Vihara and over time, this name gradually evolved into Bihar, the name of the Indian state we know today.

KNOW YOUR STATES

- Patna is the capital of Bihar. It is said to be one of the oldest cities in India.
- Chhath Puja is a major festival celebrated in Bihar, which is dedicated to the Sun God.
- Hindi is the most spoken language in Bihar. But Urdu is a close second, as are the languages Bhojpuri and Maithili.
- Aryabhata, the ancient mathematician and astronomer, was from Bihar.
- India's first president, Dr. Rajendra Prasad, was from Bihar.
- Bihar is home to one of the first residential universities in the world, the Nalanda University.
- The ancient Nanda empire, Maurya empire, and Gupta empire were founded in what is known as present-day Bihar.
- Bihar is famous for Madhubani or Mithila painting, a colourful folk art made using natural colours and beautiful patterns.

5

CHHATTISGARH

The Land of Thirty-Six Garhs

In ages past, in a time period known as the Treta Yuga, there was a prince called Rama. He was the human incarnation of God. Prince Rama would go on to marry Sita. He would battle Ravana, the most powerful demon king that the world had ever seen. His story would end up becoming so famous that people far beyond the borders of his land would hear of it. But that was for the future, because this is a story of a land he thought of with the fondest of memories – a land that his mother grew up in. Back then, this land was called Dakshin Kosala. Prince Rama's mother, Kausalya, was the princess of this land before she got married and left for the great kingdom of Ayodhya. She never cut her ties with her land though, bringing her son, Rama, to visit it whenever possible. Prince Rama loved exploring the dense forests in Dakshin

Kosala and wandering along the banks of the many rivers that flowed there.

When Rama grew up and had children of his own, he wanted his sons to be able to take care of and protect the land that he had always loved. He placed his younger son, Kusha, on the throne of Dakshin Kosala. King Kusha took wonderful care of the land and helped preserve the forests and the people who lived in its towns and villages. During King Kusha's reign, and later under his descendants, the land came to be known as a warm and welcoming place that would shelter anyone who was in need.

Time kept passing as it always does, and the Treta Yuga gave way to the Dvapara Yuga, the next cycle of time according to the ancient Hindu way of time keeping. In the north of the land, where Prince Rama spent his childhood and his younger son had once ruled, there was a kingdom called Magadha. It was now the time of the great Kurukshetra War, which was later written about in the epic Mahabharata. Magadha was ruled by a powerful king called Jarasandha. Jarasandha was not a king who believed in peace. He was said to have the strength of ten thousand elephants. His weapon of choice was a mace, and he was able to throw it to very far distances.

He believed in getting his way by any means necessary. Jarasandha attacked all the neigbouring kingdoms as a way to make his land even bigger. Many kings tried to stop him or defend themselves and their kingdoms from being annexed by him. Some kingdoms had been attacked so many times that they had moved their capital city to another city in the stealth of the night, just to avoid going on war with him.

Jarasandha showed no mercy to the kings he defeated. He imprisoned them in chains and brought them back to his kingdom where he threw them all into dungeons. The day came when Jarasandha's dungeons were filled with eighty-six kings. Jarasandha made it known in the palace that the day he filled the dungeons with a hundred kings, all hundred of the kings would be killed.

The people of Jarasandha's kingdom were unhappy with the way their king was ruling. He had already attacked and annexed the defeated kings' lands. What was the need to be so cruel? And if he could treat royalty like that, what would he do to the common man who did not agree with what was happening? The wealthy and powerful, the ministers and nobility, possibly even the warriors and merchants, would be safe. But what about the rest of the common folk who lived there?

People started having secret meetings, making plans to move far away from the land they were born in. It was time to move to a land known for the well-being of the people and for sheltering those in need. As the days passed and Jarasandha continued on his rampage, the people of his kingdom started fleeing to other lands, hoping to come back once Jarasandha was finally defeated by someone stronger than him.

In the cover of the night, thirty-six families from Jarasandha's kingdom made their way to Dakshina Kosala. They crossed rivers and stayed overnight in jungles. And finally, after walking for weeks and weeks,

the thirty-six families made it to Dakshina Kosala. All the families were treated with utmost kindness and compassion. They were given plots of land to set up their homes, cultivate their fields, and graze their cows. The thirty-six families were overjoyed, and they started building their new life in this land, where they could live free of fear.

Years later, they heard that the evil King Jarasandha had been killed in battle by Bhima, the strongest of the Pandavas. That night, the eldest members of each of the thirty-six families met to discuss whether they wanted to return to where they had come from. But each of them considered the new lives they had built, and the warmth of the community they were surrounded by, and decided that this was their home now. The land that had welcomed the thirty-six families would now be the homeland for not just them but for their descendants as well.

What does this have to do with Chhattisgarh, you might ask? Do you know that the word for thirty-six in Hindi is *chhattis*? Legend says that the land that was once Dakshina Kosala was named Chhattisgarh after the thirty-six families that moved here and built a new home or *garh* in this compassionate land, and that is what the state was called ever after.

KNOW YOUR STATES

- Chhattisgarh is known as the Tribal heart of India. The state is famous for its large tribal population and deep-rooted tribal culture.
- Raipur is the capital of Chhattisgarh. There are many stories on how Raipur got its name. A popular one is about a prince called Brahmdeo Rai establishing a new capital city that was named Raipur in his honour.
- The language spoken in Chhattisgarh is called Chhattisgarhi. It is also known as Dakshin Kosali or Kosali.
- The state of Chhattisgarh was formed in the year 2000, when it was separated from Madhya Pradesh.
- The main folk dances of the state are Panthi, Rawat Nacha, and Saila.
- Chhattisgarh is home to India's widest water fall called the Chitrakote Falls.
- Chhattisgarh is known for its Tussar silk.
- The state is famous for the Barnawapara Wildlife Sanctuary that provides shelter to leopards, porcupines, antelopes, and other wild animals.

6

GOA

The Land Once Known as Govapuri

This story is about a land that lies hugging the sea, probably because it remembers when the sea covered it like a blanket. A land that was under the protection of the god of the seas, Varuna. But the fate of the land was not just to be a home for sea creatures of all kinds. Its destiny was to flourish and prosper under the gaze of the bright sun. When this land was still part of the sea floor, a warrior priest called Parashurama came to the mountains that bordered this land. He was looking for a place where he could conduct a puja. After the religious ceremony, he wanted to bring along a group of learned families to live on this land and take care of it. Parashurama stood on the mountain and spun around, looking for a piece of land that would work for his purposes. But wherever he looked, all he could see was the sea.

Parashurama closed his eyes and meditated on the god of the seas, Varuna. 'Oh god of the seas, I need some land. I request you to move back and give me some of the land that is under your protection. I promise that my people will take care of it,' he prayed.

The response came in the form of aggressive waves crashing further up the coast, almost touching the foothills of the mountains that Parashurama was standing on. Parashurama was known for being short-tempered. He had asked the god nicely, but the god, instead of responding, had gruffly pushed forward. Parashurama saw red. He closed his eyes, picked up his bow, and placed an arrow in it. Parashurama took a deep breath and pointed his arrow up at the sky and then at the sea. If Varuna did not give up his land on his own, then Parashurama would take it by force. He twanged his bow, pulled the arrow back, and let it fly. The arrow whooshed away with the force of an earthquake. It met its target right in the middle of the sea. The sea waves recoiled in absolute shock and ran back, revealing a perfect plot of land with golden sands. Parashurama immediately claimed the land that would soon be called Banali, which in the classical language of Sanskrit meant 'the village where the arrow landed.'

Parashurama was successful in bringing over people to live in this new land.

As time passed, the land became known for its lovely beaches and playful waves. The people of the land – men, women, and children – loved to swim in the sea and build sandcastles on its shores. The land that had been reclaimed from the sea was so fertile that it had coconut trees and long patches of grass, perfect for cows to graze in. Many people had moved here from other kingdoms, excited by the beauty, the sunshine, and the seas lapping at the shores. A lot of people had started new lives here as cow herders. The cows would happily walk through the grass, munching and chewing as their caretakers splashed in the waters of the sea.

It was at a happy time like this that Lord Krishna, the king of Mathura, the leader of the Yadavas, and the god of love and compassion, visited this land that was reclaimed from the sea. As he walked on the shore, his bare feet enjoying the feeling of the golden sands sinking a little to bear his weight, his eyes fell on the people enjoying themselves in the waters. It was a group of joyful women, their beauty enhanced by how happy they were. Krishna was so charmed by the sight of their happiness that he wanted to play a song on his flute for them. He immediately took out his flute, that he carried with him everywhere, and started playing a beautiful melody.

Charmed by the song, everyone around came over to listen to him as if in a trance. Krishna kept playing and the people started dancing around him as anyone who listened to his music always did. But then to the people's wonder, the cows grazing nearby came to Krishna and lovingly nuzzled his neck and shoulder. Krishna loved it when animals responded to his music. He kept playing till the whole land was wrapped in the warm embrace of his music.

Before Krishna travelled onwards to the next land, he gave this land where he had found so much joy and happiness a name. He named it Govapuri, or the land of the *gopis* and *gopikas*, the men and women who protected the *gos*, as cows were called in Sanskrit. Lord Krishna also promised that he would always be

there to protect the land in his form as Lord Govnath. The stories say that Lord Krishna was so refreshed after visiting the land he named Govapuri that he proclaimed that Govapuri was like a paradise on earth. He said that just one glance at Govapuri was enough to cleanse one of their sins and that there was no land that could compare to this land that was once part of the sea.

As time passed, the name of Govapuri was affectionately shortened by the people who lived there. It became Gove in Kannada, Govā in Marathi, and Goy in Konkani, the last being the language spoken by the majority of people who live there. Through all these variations, Govapuri became the Goa that we know today.

KNOW YOUR STATES

- Goa celebrates two independence days. One on 15 August 1947, with the rest of the country. However, Goa was ruled by the Portuguese as a colony for almost 450 years, struggling for their liberation even as the rest of India earned its freedom. The people of Goa had to fight for another fourteen years to throw off the shackles of foreign rule. Finally, on 19 December 1961, the Indian Armed Forces liberated the state from the Portuguese, giving the state its freedom.
- The capital of Goa is Panaji. According to historians, the old name of this land was Pahajani Khali. Some say that it was also called Panji or Ponji, which meant 'land that never gets flooded,' in the local language. When the Portuguese took control over the land, they renamed it Panjim. After liberation in 1961, the name was changed back to Panaji.
- Goa is India's smallest state by area.
- Goa's food is a unique mix of Indian and Portuguese flavors, famous for dishes like vindaloo, sorpotel, and delicious seafood.
- Goa is home to more than 400 species of birds.

7

GUJARAT

The Land of the Invincible Gurjaras

Legend says that thousands of years ago, there was a land called Pancasara. It was ruled by a fair and just king called King Jayashikara. Pancasara was such a great land to live in that all the kingdoms on all sides of Pancasara came to hear the stories of its wonderful king and fortunate people. According to the stories, living in the land of Pancasara was so wonderful that no one even dreamt of paradise anymore. The kings and queens of the neighbouring kingdoms were furious when they heard that their own people were now talking about moving to King Jayashikara's land. So angered was King Bhuvada, king of a land called Kanakauja, that he decided to go to war against King Jayashikara.

The armies of both kingdoms met on the battlefield. After weeks of sword fights and bow and arrow battles, and fights with maces and spears, the war ended.

King Jayashikara won the war and brought glory and honour to Pancasara. The bitter and defeated king of Kanakauja went back home to his kingdom. But he was not done yet. King Bhuvada was already plotting his next move against King Jayashikara. King Jayashikara was happy that he had won the war, but he, too, knew that his enemy would not remain silent for long. What would happen to his kingdom if they were attacked again? He had to plan for the future.

King Jayashikara called on his wife, Queen Rupasundari, who had always stood by his side and helped him rule the kingdom. He also called on her brother Surapala and told them he was worried that another war might be imminent. Queen Rupasundari listened to him calmly, her face never showing any emotions, even though she was concerned inside. She was a brave woman, and was using all her reserves of courage to give King Jayashikara the confidence he needed. Her brother Surapala was one the best warriors in Pancasara's army, and he was now looking at her with his eyebrows knitted together. You see, the queen was about to have a baby, an heir to the throne of Pancasara. What would happen to the baby if King Jayashikara and the army were defeated in battle? The three of them sat together and decided what to do. If the king was to fall in battle, the queen had to make sure that their infant remained hidden and that Surapala would have to raise the child.

Sadly, King Jayashikara's predictions came true. King Bhuvada declared war on Pancasara for the second time. Both armies met again, weary after the last battle but determined to do their best for their lands. After weeks of intense battle, King Jayashikara fell, and Pancasara was lost. Back in the palace, Queen Rupasundari had given birth to a baby boy. She knew the enemy hordes were advancing towards the capital city. Queen Rupasundari tied her baby onto herself with a shawl made from the beautiful Patola fabric. She jumped on her horse and sped towards the jungle. She found the tallest tree and quickly tied a hammock on its branches with the same Patola she had used to wrap the baby to herself. Then Queen Rupasundari placed the baby in the hammock, prayed that her brother would find him soon and jumped back onto her horse. She had to defend the palace and the rest of the members of the royal family. Queen Rupasundari knew the forest would find a way to care for her baby boy. She had always thought of the forest like a friend and a guardian. The tall, ancient trees had watched over countless generations who had grown up in this land, irrespective of their wealth or status. The babbling streams that ran through the forest, the whispering leaves, and the protective branches of the trees were all magical to her. She trusted the forest with all her heart. As she rode away, she knew that the forest would know the best way to nurture and nourish her baby and the future king.

Later that day, a monk named Silagunasuri was passing through the forest on his way to the monastery when he noticed that the tallest tree in the woods was not bending to the force of the wind as it usually did.

Silagunasuri realized that the forest was protecting someone by letting the tree stand upright. He climbed the tree, found the baby, and instantly recognized it as the royal heir because of the richness of the fabric of the hammock he was in. The monk carefully carried the baby down and took him to his monastery. He decided to take care of the baby with some other monks and a nun called Viramati.

Meanwhile, Surapala, the queen's brother, had escaped from the battlefield with his life. He, too, had turned to the forests to live his life as a bandit. Surapala made it to the monastery, where he told the monks that he would take charge of the baby's physical training when he grew up if the monks and the nun took care of the rest. Together, they named the baby Vanaraja, or the King of the Forest.

Vanaraja grew up in the forests, being trained in multiple arts and disciplines by his uncle and the inhabitants of the monastery. He showed particular skill in archery and was skilled in debate as well. He charmed everyone he met, and everyone knew that he would be a wonderful leader when he finally got the opportunity.

When Vanaraja grew old enough to work, he started approaching the rich and wealthy merchants of the area. They appointed him as the leader in charge of money and fee collections. Vanaraja did his job well and amassed many supporters over the years. Supporters were ready to fight and decimate the enemy for him. According to legend, the people prepared to fight for him were called Gurjaras from the ancient Sanskrit, where *gur* meant 'enemy' and *jar* meant 'destroyer.'

The Gurjaras were known as a warrior community whose tales had been told in the Ramayana and the Mahabharata. With the Gurjaras on his side, Vanaraja had nothing to fear. He consolidated them into an army and marched back to his kingdom. Then, after a swift battle, Vanaraja reclaimed the throne and expanded his territories. The Gurjaras who had fought with him and for him spread across the length and breadth of the land. And to honour this warrior tribe, the land of Vanaraja came to be known as Gurjaratra or the 'land of the invincible Gurjaras.' And from this came the name we know today, Gujarat.

KNOW YOUR STATES

- Gujarat is known as the Land of the Lions. The state is home to the Asiatic lion found in the Gir forest.
- The capital of Gujarat is Gandhinagar. It was named in honour of Mahatma Gandhi, who was born in Porbandar, a seaport in the state.
- Gujarati is the official language of Gujarat.
- Gujarat has the longest coastline in India. It is around 1,600 kilometres long.
- India's first Marine National Park is in the Gulf of Kutch in Gujarat.
- Gujarat hosts an international kite festival in Ahmedabad every year.
- Gujarat is home to the Great Rann of Kutch, the largest salt desert in the world! It looks like a huge white blanket stretching as far as the eye can see.
- Gujarat is home to the Statue of Unity, the tallest statue in the world! It's built in honour of Sardar Vallabhbhai Patel, a great leader of India.

8

HARYANA

The Land of Hari or God

This legend is from many, many millennia ago, before the universe as we know it existed. All that existed was a vast, dark cosmic ocean with no sun or moon or planets or stars. Within this motionless dark ocean that was neither hot nor cold, there lay a golden egg, and the seed of all creation was hidden within it. When the time came for the cosmos to branch out into the universe and life itself, the golden egg floated to the surface. A thin crack slowly formed, and the egg started to glow and vibrate. The glow grew and grew as the vibration became louder and louder, till with a loud Om sound, the egg cracked, and Lord Brahma, the creator, was born.

It was now up to him to create the universe as we know it today. But no creation was possible without knowledge, so the first thing Lord Brahma did was to create the goddess of wisdom, Saraswati. Now, armed with the power of knowledge, Lord Brahma started the process of creation. He made air, fire, earth, and water, and they all shaped themselves into outer space and stars and oceans and rivers and the planets, including earth itself. Now, he needed a place to create the living beings that would populate all the realms.

Lord Brahma searched across the universe. And that is when his gaze fell upon a beautiful land on earth. It was bordered by two rivers, one of which he recognized as waters blessed by Goddess Saraswati herself. This was where he would complete the creation of the universe. Lord Brahma descended to earth and settled himself near a vast water body, so huge that it looked like a sea even though it was not. Lord Brahma set up an altar, called upon fire to purify it, and conducted a ceremony known as a yajna. The yajna needed the presence of the other two gods of the Trinity to succeed. So, Lord Brahma dedicated a temple to Lord Shiva, the destroyer, in the middle of the water. He invited Lord Vishnu, the preserver, to join him in the water and bless it to make it as sacred as his heavenly abode. By the end of the ceremony, Lord Brahma had created the rest of the universe with the powers of preservation, destruction, and knowledge by his side. Before he ascended back to the heavens, he, too, blessed the water to wash away the sins of those who took a dip in it. The place was later known as Brahma Sarovar, and the land was called Bhramavarta, a land where gods and goddesses would continue to visit through time.

As years passed, the fame of the holy water grew, and the land became home to the dynasty of the Kurus, transforming the name to Kurukshetra. All the kings and queens of the Kuru line continued caring for Brahma Sarovar and the Shiva temple in the middle of the water, which was said to be especially powerful during the solar eclipse. Those who took a dip in it then were said to be rewarded with many blessings.

Legend says that many years later, the Kurus split into the Pandavas and the Kauravas. The cousins went to war against each other on this sacred land of Kurukshetra. As the war raged on, Arjuna, the Pandava, found that he could not bring himself to go to war against his cousins and elders of his family. So, Lord Krishna, his friend and the king of Dwaraka, advised Arjuna to perform as was his duty. Lord Krishna said that it was Arjuna's duty to live his life with integrity and honesty. This advice is said to have been given under a banyan tree on the Kurukshetra battlefield, and later, all that Lord Krishna said to Arjuna was compiled as the Bhagavad Gita.

Arjuna took Krishna's advice to heart and stepped up and fought. The war stretched on for eighteen days. Towards the end of the war, the leader of the Kauravas, Duryodhana, searched for a place to hide and rest for a while from the fight. And the place that he chose was the Brahma Sarovar. As long as he hid there, he knew he would be safe, for in the eyes of the gods, no one who asked for protection

would be turned away. The story of this war between the Kauravas and the Pandavas on the sacred land of Kurukshetra is what we know today as the great Indian epic, the Mahabharata.

Once the war ended, Kurukshetra returned to times of peace. Memories of the battles and bloodshed faded, and all that remained were the memories of those divine entities that had passed through these sacred grounds. A goddess who had flowed through these lands as a river. A god who created a universe and yet another who still dwelled in the water of the Brahma Sarovar. And a god who advised a warrior in the middle of the battlefield and gave all humans the best principles to live by. With so much association with the gods, the people who lived here believed that only the truly good could be born here. They started holding themselves to a divine code, behaving only in the best possible way, as if the gods themselves had told them how to live. This land came to be known as Haryana. In Sanskrit, *Hari*, means 'God', and *ayana*, means 'abode or home'. Together, Hari-ayana means 'the abode of Hari or God', which over time became Haryana.

KNOW YOUR STATES

- Haryana is often called the 'Milk Pail of India.' While other states also produce a lot of milk, Haryana has the largest number of people working in dairy farming. The state has a strong dairy tradition and is famous for special animals like the Murrah buffalo.
- Chandigarh is the capital of Haryana. It shares this capital with the neighbouring state of Punjab. Don't forget to read how Chandigarh got its name in the chapter on union territories in the book.
- Some of the most popular forms of musical theatre in Haryana are Saang, Rasa Lila, and Ragini.
- Haryana is famous for its rich sporting culture, especially wrestling. It is called Kushti. Haryana is known for producing many top athletes and Olympians, especially in wrestling, boxing, and kabaddi.
- One of the most loved dishes from Haryana is the Bajra Khichdi, which is made with millets and lentils.

9

HIMACHAL PRADESH

The Land of the Snowy Mountains

Long, long ago, a mighty flood swept across the Earth. The entire planet was submerged under deep sea, with not even an inch of land allowed to peek out. High up in the heavens, the gods and goddesses watched as the Earth tried to shake herself dry. It took thousands of years, but finally, the Earth rocked and sent tremors across her surface till the land covered by the sea waters pushed its way out. The land that rose up to the surface was not just flat, though. Some parts were tall, and some parts were deep. Some parts had the sandy floor of the oceans, and some had the darkest of soil. And then, some parts of the land started rising upwards to the heavens. Higher and higher, the land rose till it touched the skies. The gods and goddesses looked at this elevated land that had folded itself into peaks and valleys. It was adorned with snow that wrapped around the mountains and valleys like a blanket of the whitest clouds. Dotted around the land were lakes and rivers that shimmered and sparkled in the sunlight like precious gems. These were the tallest mountains to ever grace the planet. The gods and goddesses could not stop exclaiming over their beauty, and some decided to make them their home. And so, the first name the land ever got was Devabhoomi, or 'the abode of the gods.'

A magnificent king named Himaraja was the heart and soul of these mountains, ruling over every snowy ridge and icy cave. People called him this because *hima* was their word for snow, and *raja* was the word for king, making him truly the 'snow king.' Himaraja was a warm and patient king who strived to do his best for all his subjects and anyone who wished to visit his kingdom. The gods and goddesses were so pleased with Himaraja that they wanted him to have a partner who could match his spirit. So, they all paid a visit to the ancient forefathers called Pitrs, who were the ancestral gods of all those who had ever lived. They asked the Pitrs to get their daughter Menawati married to Himaraja.

Like Himaraja, Menawati, too, was the living heart of a mountain within Himaraja's kingdom. Menawati was happy to get married to Himaraja. The wedding was celebrated with great pomp and grandeur high up on the peaks of Himaraja's kingdom. All the gods and goddesses attended and enjoyed the festivities, blessing King Himaraja and Queen Menawati. The spirits of the forests, called Yakshas and Yakshis, came to visit the newlywed couple and presented them with many exquisite treasures. The deities of the rivers and lakes promised to live in their land, blessing their people for as long as there was 'Hima,' or snow, on the peaks of the mountains.

King Himaraja and Queen Menawati were happy in their kingdom, nestled at the foothills of the snow-covered mountains. They were often visited by Goddess Sati, Lord Shiva's beloved, and Menawati cared for her as if Sati were her own daughter. When Sati stopped coming to the mountains, both Himaraja and Menawati missed her presence. They wondered why she was not seen on the snowy slopes anymore. Much later, they were visited by a heartbroken Shiva who told them that Sati was no more. Lord Shiva asked Himaraja if he could stay there in Himaraja's kingdom and meditate to mend his broken heart. Himaraja immediately agreed and promised to keep the world away by creating impassable snowy cliffs and ravines. Lord Shiva climbed to the top of a mountain peak called Kailasa and settled in to meditate.

Many years passed, and one day, King Himaraja and Queen Menawati were summoned by all the deities in heaven. They were told Sati would be reborn on Earth, so Lord Shiva could reunite with her. She would take the form of the mother goddess and be born to King Himaraja and Queen Menawati. Both the king and the queen were overjoyed. When their daughter was born, they named her Parvati, which means 'daughter of the mountain king.' As the gods and goddesses had predicted, Parvati grew up wanting to reunite with Shiva. There was only one problem, though, Shiva was still lost in meditation at the top of Mount Kailasa.

But then the king of gods, Indra, summoned the god and goddess of love, Kamadeva and Rati Devi, to wake up Lord Shiva from his meditation. Kamadeva shot Lord Shiva with one of his arrows made of sugarcane, and Lord Shiva woke up to see Parvati standing in front of him. He immediately recognized Sati's spirit in her. Himaraja was overjoyed to see his daughter unite with her true love. Shiva and Parvati decided to live in Mount Kailash and make the mountains their home. Other gods and goddesses, too, chose to make the mountains of Himaraja their home. Kubera, the god of wealth and the Yakshas, decided to build his kingdom there. Goddess Saraswati, the goddess of wisdom, transformed into a river that began her journey to other lands from these mountains.

King Himaraja and Queen Menawati decided to leave the mountains for the gods. They remained in their kingdom, which flourished and prospered in the shade of these glittering peaks. The people of their kingdom knew that life was this beautiful despite the icy cold of the snow because of the warmth and compassion of Himaraja and his queen. As Himaraja faded into the pages of myths and legends, the land known as the 'king of snow's kingdom' became known as the 'land of snowy mountains' or Himachal Pradesh, where the word *hima* means 'snow,' *achal* means 'slopes,' and *pradesh* means 'land.'

KNOW YOUR STATES

- Himachal Pradesh is known as the Apple State of India because of its large apple orchards and important role in apple production.
- Shimla is the capital of Himachal Pradesh. During British rule, the town of Shimla was designated as the summer capital of the British. The name Shimla is said to have been derived from the word 'Shymalaya,' meaning 'Blue House,' which was the name of a house built with blue slate. This house was said to have been built by a fakir in Jakhu. Another story goes that the name Shimla comes from 'Shymala,' which means 'Blue woman,' which was another name for Goddess Kali.
- The snow leopard is the state animal of Himachal Pradesh. These magnificent animals can be spotted in the Kibber Wildlife Sanctuary.
- Built in 1893, the Chail Cricket Ground located in the state is said to be the highest cricket ground in the world.
- Himachal Pradesh is home to one of Asia's largest glaciers known as Bara Shigri.

10

JHARKHAND

The Land of the Forests

Nestled in the eastern part of the historic Indian subcontinent is the land known as Jharkhand. Jharkhand is the land of *jal* (water), *jangal* (forest), and *jamin* (land). The first ever inhabitants of this gem of a forested land with its mountains, waterfalls, and rivers were the Adivasis, the original inhabitants. The Adivasis of Jharkhand were also known as the Santals. Now, many, many thousands of years ago, when the Santals themselves had just begun living in the forests, they used to be a nomadic tribe. They would travel from place to place within the forest, never leaving its warm embrace as they hunted for food and a safe place to spend the night. Every evening, all of them would find a tree or a grove of trees to settle down in its shade to rest. Before they made themselves comfortable, they would thank every leaf on the tree and on the ground, and they would say thank you to every drop of water nearby and every inch of earth that they stepped on. The Santals lived in deep harmony with nature.

The story goes that one day a group of Santals went into the forest to look for food. They were carrying their bows and arrows to protect themselves from danger. As they walked deeper and deeper into the forest, one Santal asked the group a rather interesting question.

'Who do you think the creator of our land is?'

The rest of the group stopped to listen to him.

'I mean, every time we stop for the night, we thank the leaves, the land, the water, and the earth, but who are we thanking? Who is our creator and our saviour?'

It was an interesting question and one that had not been asked before. The group decided to postpone the journey and think about the answer instead.

One of the Santals said, 'I believe that the sun is the creator. The sun shines light on the land for us and takes the darkness away. The sun brings us warmth when it is cold. The sun helps us light fires with dried-up leaves. The sun probably created us all.'

Some nodded in agreement, while some crinkled up their noses and shook their heads.

'You might be right, but the sun also burns us sometimes and dries up all our water. Would a saviour do that?' one of the Santals, who had shaken his head, asked.

The group thought about that for a minute. The questioner was right.

'Then how about the cloud? The cloud brings us rain when the sun dries up the water. The cloud gives us shade when the sun burns us,' another member of the group responded.

'Yes, all that is true. But the cloud does not give us light. And what use is a cloud in the night?' the one who had suggested the sun responded.

'What about the wind then?' another Santal asked.

'The wind is stronger than the clouds. It can blow it away. When the clouds stubbornly stay away, the wind brings it in our direction. When the sun burns us up, the wind blows and cools us down. The wind is truly one of our protectors,' said yet another Santal.

'That might be true, but the wind also blows our scent to dangerous beings in the forest. That is how they sense us sometimes. Would a true saviour really do that?'

The Santals started arguing amongst themselves, the hunger long forgotten, till one of them loudly clapped his hands for silence.

'I have a plan,' he announced.

'Let us send an arrow out into the sky. The arrow has always pointed us in the right direction to find our food or settle for the night. The arrow will also help us find the right answer in this case. What do you all think?'

The rest of the group agreed. They all stood in a circle and got their best archer to stand in the middle. He closed his eyes for a moment to concentrate and then shot the arrow off into the sky.

'Look how high the arrow is going. The wind is pushing it forward,' one of them called out.

'But look how the arrow passed through the clouds. Was that the arrow telling us that the cloud is the real creator?' another one asked.

'But see how the sun glints on the arrow and makes it shine. It is surely a sign,' some of them said, nodding their heads.

The arrow that had been going straight up until then abruptly changed course and started coming back down. Speedily, the arrow flew as if aiming for a grove of Sal trees in the distance. The Santals started running behind it to see where it would land. They saw it fly towards the Sal grove and suddenly vanish from sight. They rushed towards the grove and came to a halt, panting, as they looked around for the arrow. Where had it gone?

Suddenly, a voice asked, 'Is this what you are looking for?'

An old woman with long flowing hair suddenly stepped out from behind a Sal tree. She was holding the arrow in her hands. As the Santals laid their eyes on her, they knew they had found the answer to their question. They immediately put their hands together and bowed to her.

'Who are you, Devi? Where did you come from?' they asked her.

The old woman smiled, and the arrow in her hand transformed into a long staff. She gestured to the grove of Sal trees behind her and simply said, 'Sarna.'

'Bless us, Sarna Devi,' the Santals said.

As they waited for her blessings with their eyes closed, the Santals remembered that they had always known they had been created and nurtured by Sarna

Devi, the spirit of the forest. Sarna Devi lived in the trees that sheltered them and in the rivers that quenched their thirst. She waved her staff to make the flowers bloom. She was the reason why the bees made honey. She blessed the children of the land, and she was the one who made the forest fruit trees bend over with fruit. Sarna Devi, their divine mother, was the forest, and the forest was her. When the Santals opened their eyes, Sarna Devi had vanished, but they knew now that she had appeared to remind them that the forest was everything to them. The Santals never forgot what the forest meant to them, and they continue to live their life protecting it. Jharkhand, the land of the Santals, too, got its name from the forest where *jhar* means 'forest' and *khand* means 'land', making Jharkhand the land of the forests.

KNOW YOUR STATES

- Jharkhand is one of India's youngest states. It was created in November 2000, with land that was previously under the administration of the state of Bihar.
- Ranchi is the capital of Jharkhand. Its name comes from the Oraon tribe. Long ago, the area was a village called 'Archi,' which means 'bamboo' in the Oraon language. There's a fun local story that a farmer once chased away a mischievous magical spirit by hitting it with a bamboo stick. The spirit shouted 'archi' three times before disappearing, and that name stayed with the place. Over time, Archi became Rachi, and then Ranchi!
- Jharkhand is known for many megalithic structures, ancient cave paintings, and burial sites.
- Chhau, Santali, and Jhumair are some of the popular folk dances from the state.
- Jharkhand is home to Saranda Forest, Asia's largest sal forest.

11

KARNATAKA

The Land on an Elevated Plain

The name of the state that we now know as Karnataka comes from a kingdom that existed long, long ago. To understand the meaning behind the name, we need to start at the very beginning, in a time shrouded in myth and legend. Many ages past, a holy man was walking along the mighty Tungabhadra River. The sage was looking for a place to meditate, a place that would bear the sign of the divine, announcing how special it truly was. As he looked to the left and the right, his gaze fell upon the most amazing sight. A giant cobra, one of the most venomous snakes, was coiled upon one of the great rocks on the banks of the river with its hood up, threatening to strike anyone that came close. However, what was most extraordinary was that the cobra was not protecting itself but a mother frog laying eggs in a pool by the rock. Watching the cobra protect a creature it would usually capture as prey made one thing clear to the holy man. It was a sign from the divine that this was sacred ground. The sage waited till the frog had safely laid all its eggs and till the cobra had slithered away.

Then he sat on that rock and meditated on the goddess of wisdom and learning, Goddess Sharadamba. The sage, whose name was Vidyaranya, ended up establishing a temple dedicated to the goddess there and a monastery where others could come and learn how to meditate and learn more about ancient scriptures. Vidyaranya's name spread far and wide across the land as time passed. People said that he was the person to seek blessings and advice from before establishing anything.

Many years after the incident with the cobra and the frog, two brothers named Harihara and Bukka ended up on the banks of the Tungabhadra on a hunting trip. Not much was known about who these brothers were or where they came from. It was rumoured that they had been generals in the army of a defeated king. Armed with hunting hounds, the brothers and their party were chasing a petrified hare who had been running away. But a few minutes into the chase, the hare stopped running. The brothers watched in shock as the hare turned around and started chasing the hounds instead.

'It's the power of the land,' a voice called out. The brothers turned around to come face to face with the famous Vidyaranya. They bowed to him and waited for him to explain what they had just seen. The holy man smiled.

'My dear boys, what you have seen is the strength of the land. This is a land that elevates the spirit of anyone who calls it home. It makes predators practise compassion. It makes prey courageous. A good land indeed,' Sage Vidyaranya said.

The brothers were inspired by his words. Harihara and Bukka had always dreamt of establishing their own kingdom. Maybe this land was where their dreams would come true. Vidyaranya agreed with them. He decided to be their advisor.

Vidyaranya told the brothers to go to the highest point of the land to dig and lay the founding stone of their empire. He would go to the neighbouring rocky outcrop and meditate for the best moment. As soon as he got a sign, he would blow his conch, and the brothers would start to dig.

Harihara and Bukka made their way to the place Vidyaranya had pointed them to and waited with their tools. As soon as they heard the sound of a conch blowing out loudly, both of them started digging to lay

the foundation. But a short while later, they heard yet another conch sound. The brothers were confused. Had they been mistaken the first time? They rushed back to their guru. He was waiting for them, and with him was a woman wearing a red sari, glowing with an unearthly energy. The brothers recognized her as Goddess Sharadamba and immediately kneeled down in front of their guru and the goddess of learning.

'I am the one who blew the conch the first time,' the goddess said. 'Your empire will flourish for sure. But there will be ups and downs. Five hundred years later, there will be another that will bear the name of your empire and prosper for thousands of years. That is how the universe has decreed it,' the goddess declared.

Harihara and Bukka took the goddess's words to heart. They went on to establish what became one of the most powerful empires that had ever existed on the land. It was named Karnatak after the 'elevated land' it was established on. The capital of the Karnatak kingdom was known as Vijayanagara or the City of Victory. Vijayanagara was so famous that artists and musicians from all over the land travelled there to be part of the kingdom. The legend goes that musicians from Vijayanagara were the ones who originated the kind of music that is now known as Carnatic music, named, of course, after the Karnatak kingdom.

Just as the goddess had prophesied, though, the Karnatak kingdom did fall after around three hundred glorious years of being a leader in architecture, arts, music, and more. But another land rose up in the dust left by the Karnatak kingdom, the Indian state of Karnataka, where the people speak the language of Kannada. The name Karnataka is derived from the Kannada words *karu* (meaning 'elevated' or 'high') and *naadu* (meaning 'land'), together referring to it as the 'elevated land'.

KNOW YOUR STATES

- The city of Mysuru in Karnataka is said to have been ruled by the demon Mahishasura. *Ooru* means city. Mahishasura ooru means 'the city of Mahishasura,' and the name Mysuru is derived from this name.
- Bengaluru is the capital of Karnataka. While there are many stories about how Bengaluru came to be named, there is one story that remains very popular. The local legend says that once a lost and hungry king was fed boiled beans by a poor old woman who took pity on him. The grateful king named the place where he was fed 'Benda-kaal-ooru' or the 'city of boiled beans.' It was this Bendakaalooru that later became Bengaluru.
- Despite being a tech city, Bengaluru is known as the Garden City of India due to its many parks and green spaces, like Lalbagh Botanical Garden and Cubbon Park.
- Karnataka is the largest exporter of coffee in the country.
- Karnataka is home to Hampi, a UNESCO World Heritage Site and also to the world's tallest freestanding monolithic statue, the Gomateshwara statue.

12

KERALA

The Land of Coconut Trees

Thousands of years ago, a warrior sage named Parashurama walked the length and breadth of the Indian subcontinent. He was known for his fury and for his unquestioning obedience towards his father, Sage Jamadagni. Like his father, Parashurama, too, believed in the power of meditation and prayers. He was devoted to Lord Shiva, the destroyer, and dedicated many years to his adoration of the god by meditating on him at a place called Gokarna. Pleased by his devotion, Lord Shiva appeared in front of him one day to gift him an axe. The axe was no ordinary weapon. It was called Vidyudhabi by the gods. The weapon had four sharp blades, and it was supposed to have supernatural powers. It had been used by Goddess Durga, one of the fiercest of the mother goddesses, in her battles. It had been used by Lord Shiva himself. The axe was also called 'Parasu.' When Lord Shiva gifted the axe to Rama, son of Sage Jamadagni, the warrior saint became Parashurama as he was known ever after. Lord Shiva knew that he could not let a man with such a terrible temper walk away with a weapon that had the power to create as well as destroy. So, he taught Parashurama the art of using the weapon wisely. He also taught Parashurama the art of defensive martial arts that would help him rein in his temper and focus his energy.

Grateful for all the gifts that he had received from Lord Shiva, Parashurama decided that he needed to honour the 108 gods and goddesses in heaven with a land worthy of divinity. He stood up on the highest peak of Gokarna and looked all around him. All that he saw was the rolling and crashing of the waves that were bordered by tall mountains. Parashurama realized that all the land he needed was stuck under the sea floor. Parashurama hoisted his axe onto his shoulder and walked to the tip of the mountain ridges. At the last tip, which was next to the sea, he closed his eyes and muttered a prayer to the sea, asking her to move back and give him some land. A giant wave splashed him defiantly as his prayer went out into the universe. Parashurama gritted his teeth. He knew what he had to do. He lifted his huge axe off his shoulder and aimed it at the sea. As if in response, the sea turned a darker shade of stormy blue, and the waves became rougher. A lesser being would have been terrified at how forbidding the sea looked. But this was Parashurama. He was scared of no being or entity. He tried requesting the sea to move back again. But she did not oblige and made her displeasure clear by sending sky-high waves. Then, Parashurama had no choice but to rotate his axe three times and send it hurtling towards the sea.

The divine Parasu flew northwards as if rushing towards Gokarna, where Lord Shiva had gifted the axe to Parashurama. Once it reached there, it fell on the ground with the force of a thousand earthquakes. The curved blade on one

side slashed through the foam and the froth of the waves and hit the sea floor with such impact that the entire sea shuddered in fear. She retreated, pulling the water and her creatures away from the weapon, leaving a brand-new sliver of land between her waves and the mountain ranges. Parashurama bounded down from the mountains to retrieve his axe and inspect the land that he wanted to dedicate to the gods.

Parashurama put a hand down and inspected the sand of this newly created land. He took some specks of sand on his index finger and gingerly tasted it. The land was salty. It was uninhabitable and one could certainly not use it to cultivate crops. Parashurama sat cross-legged on the sand and prayed to Lord Shiva for direction. He appeared to him in a vision and told him to pray to Vasuki, the snake god and king of the Nagas. Parashurama did as he was told.

Vasuki, the giant serpent who was usually found coiled around Lord Shiva's neck, agreed to help Parashurama. He and his community of Nagas gave Parashurama a special kind of venom that the warrior saint spread across the land. Once absorbed, the salty land transformed into one of the most fertile lands on the planet. Parashurama planted coconut trees, mango trees, jackfruit trees, and other plants from one tip to the other. And the land that the sea had given up became lush green, as if the gods themselves had made the land with their own hands. Parashurama was so grateful to the Nagas for their invaluable help that he appointed them as the eternal guardians of the land. He decreed that serpents and snakes would always be honoured in this land and that every ancestral home would have a serpent grove with lamps lit in the snake's honour.

Parashurama knew that even though he was immortal, he could not be around to defend the land he had reclaimed from the sea. So, once the land's first inhabitants arrived, he taught them the martial arts he learnt from Lord Shiva. His first disciples the called it Kalaripayattu, which meant 'training for the battleground.'

The legend goes that one of Parashurama's final acts was to establish a kingdom of people who called themselves Cheras. The Cheras went on to become mighty kings, and in time, the land they ruled over came to be known as Kerala. Some say the land is called Kerala because it was the Chera kingdom of the Cheras. Some say it is named Kerala because in

Malayalam (the local language) the Coconut tree is called *Kera*, thus Kerala translates to the 'land of the Coconut tree.' But others say that Kerala is named after the Malayalam word *cherna*, which means 'joined,' reminding everyone that it is a land that rose up from under the sea to join the rest of the world.

KNOW YOUR STATES

- Kerala is famous for its spices like black pepper, cardamom, and cinnamon, which have been traded worldwide for centuries.
- Thiruvananthapuram is the capital of Kerala. The city gets its name from the word *Thiru-Anantha-puram* meaning the 'city of Lord Anantha.' Anantha is the sacred serpent on which Lord Vishnu, the preserver of the Hindu Trinity, reclines.
- Kerala has the highest literacy rate in India, with around 96%, making it the most literate state in the country. In 2016, it became the first Indian state to achieve total primary education through the Athulyam programme.
- Kerala has a unique dance form called Kathakali, which is a form of storytelling through dance.
- The unique martial art form from Kerala is called Kalaripayattu.
- The state animal of Kerala is the elephant. Elephants can be seen in the wild at the elephant reserves in Wayanad, Anamudi, Periyar, and Nilambur in Kerala.

13

MADHYA PRADESH

The Land in the Centre

The words *Madhya Pradesh* literally mean 'the land in the centre of the country.' This also makes it the beating heart of the land we call India. Madhya Pradesh is home to many indigenous tribes, who are the original inhabitants of the land. Some of these tribes have been around since before the ancient Indian epics of the Mahabharata and the Ramayana. They are mentioned in these epics as communities that live in the jungle and protect it from any outsiders who might come there. The oldest of these tribes is the Baiga tribe that has lived in Madhya Pradesh for more than twenty thousand years!

When the Baigas first started living in the jungles of Madhya Pradesh, before people lived in cities or had invented cars or bicycles or books or even written language or anything really, they believed that their land was the only land where humans lived. They believed that in the earliest of times, in the time before they existed, there was only water everywhere. Now, on this endless expanse of water was a single old leaf that bobbed up and down on the waves. Lying on this leaf, relaxing and floating off to wherever the leaf took him was God. God was in no hurry to do anything. He liked the silence and the peace and quiet in this world where there was only water, him, and his leaf. But as time passed and nothing ever changed, God began to wonder whether there should be more. He looked out at the water, fluid and ever-changing, and thought that maybe this world needed something more that was solid and immovable, like land.

Making land would take a lot of work, but God knew that there were other beings who had land elsewhere. So, God decided to create something that would bring him land. He sat up on his leaf and leaned forward. Then he dipped the tip of his finger in water and then touched it to his chest to make a dark mixture. He moulded it this way and that to create a crow. Crow opened his eyes and blinked at God.

'Welcome!' God said with a smile.

'Caw, Caw! Hello!' Crow responded.

'Crow, I need you to go and find land,' God commanded Crow, and off the newly made bird flew.

Crow looked here and there for land. Finally, he saw something hard and solid in the distance. Could that be land? Crow flew down only to find out that it was hard and solid, all right, but it was the shell of a tortoise with two great tusks. Crow sighed. He was tired and needed to rest his wings. He settled down on the tortoise's shell.

'So, you are not land then?' Crow asked the tortoise in a voice filled with great exhaustion.

'No, I am Kunwar Kakarmal,' the tortoise replied in a serious voice as he continued to swim. 'But,' he continued, 'I do know where you can find some land.'

'Oh, dear Kunwar Kakarmal, do not lie to me. Tell me where I can find some land so that I can take it back,' Crow pleaded with the tortoise.

'Take a deep breath and hold on to my tusks then,' Kunwar Kakarmal said to Crow, and with that, he plunged into the waters. Onward the tortoise went till he reached Patala loka, the netherworld deep at the bottom of the waters. And lo and behold, there was all the land and all the soil there in the netherworld. It had been stolen by Raja Kichakmal, the ruler of the netherworld, who wanted to keep it all to himself.

'Please, Raja Kichakmal, I would like to take some of the land back to God,' Crow said to the ruler of the netherworld. After a moment's hesitation, he agreed and handed some soil from the land over to Crow, who jumped back onto the tortoise Kakarmal's tusks and went back to the surface of the water again.

After thanking the tortoise Kunwar Kakarmal for all his help, Crow brought the soil back to God. God patted Crow and thanked him for his service. He had known that Crow would succeed, so he had kept a few things ready as the next steps to making land.

God emptied the soil into a large vessel. Then he clapped his hands, and a large snake came slithering out of the water and jumped into God's hands. God transformed the vessel and the snake into a churner and started churning the soil in it this way and that. Once it was churned well, God stood up on his leaf and scattered it into the water. As soon as the churned soil touched the water, it spread in four directions as land.

God travelled across the land to inspect it. Would the soil be good enough for the rest of his creations? He realized that the land made of churned soil and water was solid, but it was movable as it was not anchored down anywhere. God saw that the land was shaking continuously, so he created a community of iron smelters called the Agaria.

The Agaria made four large iron nails for God and told him that these nails had the strength to anchor the land down in the north, south, east, and west. After that, God created the Nanga Baiga and the Nangi Baigi, the first Baigas ever to set foot on the land and gave them the nails. The Baigas travelled to all four corners of the land and secured the shaking of the land so well that the movement stopped, and the land became still, as it is today. God was so pleased with the work the Baigas had done that he designated them the protectors of the earth.

The story goes that as the protectors of the earth, the Baigas were to always remain on the beating heart of the land, the central region from where all of life and the earth was created. This land, which is known as the 'central region,' was named Madhya Pradesh, where *madhya* means central and *pradesh* means land.

KNOW YOUR STATES

- Madhya Pradesh is known as the Tiger State of India. The state is home to one of the most significant numbers of tiger populations and tiger habitats.
- Bhopal is the capital of Madhya Pradesh. Bhopal gets its name from the words *Bhoj Taal*, meaning Bhoj's Lake. King Bhoj was an eleventh-century king who ruled the land.
- An ancient dance form from Madhya Pradesh is the Karma dance, or Karma Naach, performed by many tribes during the autumn season.
- Madhya Pradesh has many famous monuments, including the Khajuraho group of temples, the Sanchi Stupa, and the Gwalior Fort.
- Gond art is a famous style of painting that originated from the Gond tribe of Madhya Pradesh.
- Chanderi and Maheshwari are two famous textiles from Madhya Pradesh.
- The famous Rudyard Kipling book titled *The Jungle Book* and the iconic Shere Khan are believed to be inspired by Madhya Pradesh and its jungles.

14

MAHARASHTRA
The Land of Warriors

The Indian state that is called Maharashtra has always been home to many tribes and empires. All the people who have called Maharashtra their kingdom, their abode, or their home have left their mark on this great state. No wonder that the name of the state still reminds us of all the great kings, queens, and warriors who have fought to protect this land. Legend talks about an ancient warrior class that descended from the Pandavas in the Mahabharata, who ruled over this land. These people defended the borders of their land and called themselves 'Maha Rattas' or 'great charioteers.' The Maha Rattas were ardent devotees of Goddess Bhavani, who was their supreme goddess and the eliminator of all evil.

According to ancient stories from this land, it was once terrorized by a demon named Matanga. Terrified, the people prayed to Lord Brahma, the creator of the universe. Lord Brahma, in his infinite wisdom, told the people to turn to Shakti, the mother goddess, for help. Shakti heard the people's prayers and took the form of ultimate destruction as Goddess Bhavani. Aided by her five sister goddesses – Brahmani, Vaishnavi, Kaumari, Indrani, and Sambhaavi – Goddess Bhavani appeared on the battlefield. Armed with many weapons, her eyes blazing, she faced the demon Matanga, whom even the gods were scared to face. Bravely using all her skills as a warrior, she wielded her weapons and vanquished the demon, bringing people to the land. Goddess Bhavani was worshipped by the people of the land for her warrior skills.

Many years after the goddess vanquished Matanga and other demons, the people who were once known as the Maha Rattas came to be known as the Marathas. Their leader at the time was Shivaji Maharaj, who would later be crowned as Chhatrapati Shivaji Maharaj. Ever since he was a young boy, Shivaji Maharaj was said to have dreamt of building a powerful empire led by the Marathas. When he was a young boy of sixteen, he seized an enemy fort and embarked on his lifelong goal of building and expanding the Maratha empire.

According to Maratha lore, Shivaji Maharaj had the blessing of Goddess Bhavani for all his military campaigns. Shivaji Maharaj's mother was believed to be an ardent devotee of the goddess as well. The legend goes that Shivaji Maharaj was involved in an arduous battle when he had an encounter of sorts with Goddess Bhavani. On the day his troops were to clash with the enemy army, Shivaji Maharaj assembled them all in front of him. Once he had their attention, Shivaji showed them his sword, which he said was named the Bhavani after the goddess. Shivaji said that the warrior Goddess Bhavani had come to him in his dreams and promised him success against his enemies. His warrior troops were inspired by Shivaji's divine inspiration, and they went on to win the battle against their enemies.

Shivaji went on to build the Maratha empire battle by battle. As the Maratha kingdom expanded, the gaze of the Mughal emperor fell upon Shivaji, and he ended up being held back in the Mughal fort in Agra under false pretexts. But no one was a match for the great Maratha who escaped from the guards of Agra fort in a fruit basket.

When Shivaji Maharaj was on a battle campaign to win over Sinhagad fort, the crown of valour was passed on to the military commander Tanaji Malusare. Sinhagad fort was on a high ridge, and the only way to get to it without the enemy noticing was by scaling a steep cliff. Legend says that Tanaji thought of a military strategy that no one had ever considered. He used Shivaji Maharaj's pet monitor lizard called Yashwanti to turn the tide. Tanaji attached a rope to the animal and made it climb up the walls. But not alone. The commander held on to the rope and scaled the impossibly high and challenging cliff to make it into

enemy territory. The battle was won, and the Marathas conquered the fort.

In yet another story about the Marathas, the mantle of greatness rests on the shoulders of a milkmaid. Shivaji Maharaj's capital was in a fort in Raigad that was high up a mountain. For the security of the people within the fort, it opened its gates at dawn and then shut them at dusk. No one could go in or out once the gates were shut. Now, one of the people who visited the capital every day was a milkmaid named Hirakani. Hirakani had a small baby who she would leave in her home at the base of the mountain.

One day, she got late at home and was late to start her day of work. She was stuck inside the fort when the gates shut. She pleaded with the guards to think of her baby and to open the gates for her. But rules are rules, they said, and refused to let her out. The milkmaid cried her heart out thinking of her baby alone at home. But then she wiped her tears. After all, she was a Maratha too. She walked towards the back of the fort, where there were no gates or walls, just a sheer drop towards the rocks below. She tightened her sari, thought of her baby, asked Goddess Bhavani for her blessing, and started climbing down. The next day, when the guards opened the gates, Hirakani, the milkmaid, was right there, battered and scratched but ready with her milk for the people of the fort. The guards were angered at the thought of her breaching their security, so they took her to Shivaji Maharaj. Instead of being angry, the king of the Marathas applauded the milkmaid for her bravery and built a wall dedicated to her at the fort instead.

As the Maratha empire spread its borders, so did the fables and legends of the courageous warrior race of the Marathas. The land of the Marathas flourished and came to be known as a fertile ground for people carrying greatness in them. As time passed, the land itself stood for greatness and was called Maharashtra, a name that came from the combination of *maha*, from the Sanskrit *mahat* meaning 'great,' and *rashtra*, meaning 'nation' or dominion.

KNOW YOUR STATES

- Maharashtra is also known as the Gateway of India. The state is home to Mumbai, which was a historically important port of entry for trade and travel.
- Mumbai is the capital of Maharashtra. The name Mumbai is derived from Goddess Mumbadevi, the patron goddess of the Koli community native to this region. The goddess is also known as Mumba or Maha Amba. Much before India's independence and during the colonial period, the Portuguese called the city Bombaim, meaning 'good bay' in their language. Bombay was what the British called the city. In 1995, it was renamed Mumbai.
- Maharashtra is the only state with a saline soda lake called the Lonar lake, which was created 52,000 years ago after a meteor hit the earth.
- Maharashtra is home to many UNESCO World Heritage sites like Ajanta Caves, Ellora Caves, Elephanta Caves, and the Chhatrapati Shivaji Maharaj Terminus.

15

MANIPUR

The Land of the Gem

The story of Manipur begins many millennia ago with a heavenly dance that even the gods yearned to see. Back in those days when gods and goddesses roamed all the realms like mortals, Lord Krishna, the god of compassion, protection, and love, was known to play his flute and dance with his Gopis. He had grown up in Vrindavan surrounded by a community of cowherds called Gopis who adored him unconditionally. Krishna showed his love for them by dancing with them through the night, filled with joy. This dance was called the Rasa Lila, and every time Krishna danced with his Gopis, waves of divine love spread through the universe.

Legend says that one night, Krishna was dancing the Rasa Lila with his beloved Radha and his Gopis, and he asked Lord Shiva to keep watch so that he could perform the Rasa Lila without the fear of being interrupted. Lord Shiva agreed to keep watch with his back to the performance.

As Shiva stood watch, his wife, Goddess Parvati, passed by. She raised an eyebrow at the curious sight. Heavenly music was wafting through the air from the clearing behind Shiva, but he had his back to it. Parvati knew that her husband loved to dance, just like she did. She approached him and asked him what he was guarding. Shiva smiled at his wife's curiosity. He never kept any secrets from her. They were both two sides of one whole. So, he let her stand behind him and watch in silence. Goddess Parvati stood and absorbed it all. After watching Krishna and the Gopis, Parvati felt moved to perform the Rasa Lila herself.

Parvati told Shiva that she wanted to dance the Rasa Lila with him. Shiva, also known as Nataraja or the god of dance, readily agreed. But he did not want to replicate the dance in their abode. Shiva wanted to make sure that he found the perfect place for them to perform the dance. Shiva embarked on a search of the three worlds to find the best place possible. There were many places that were beautiful and welcoming, but none matched the vision that Shiva and Parvati had in their minds. Finally, after moving on from one beautiful location after another, Shiva chanced upon a gorgeous lake surrounded by green and thickly forested mountains. It gleamed under the morning sun like a freshly polished gem. Despite its beauty, it was secluded, and Shiva could just envision dancing the Rasa Lila here with his wife.

Shiva raised up his trident and struck the gleaming lake with it. The lake shimmered and stretched out into a river with multiple branches. The water then started emptying out into three underground caves that had opened up at the foothills of Chinghungut mountain that stood bordering the lake that no longer was. As the water drained out of the basin, it revealed the most beautiful valley that Shiva had ever seen. Now, he had a location where he could dance the Rasa Lila with Parvati.

Shiva stood in the centre of the valley and experimentally did a few steps. It was perfect as a stage, but to truly do the Rasa Lila, he would need the accompaniments as well. Shiva closed his eyes and thought back to the night he had stood guard. He had heard the drums called Mrudangas, the flute of Krishna, and the *ghungroo*s or the musical anklets of the dancers. What were some instruments he needed to make his Rasa Lila evoke the same feeling? The single-stringed instrument called the Pena, and the drum called the Pung were chosen for the music. Shiva asked the celestial beings called the Gandharvas to use the instruments and create the music that Parvati and he would dance to.

Now, with the stage set and preparations done, Shiva invited Parvati to this newly created valley that rivalled all other places on earth with its natural beauty and quiet radiance. To honour the silence and the land, Parvati and Shiva danced their version of the Rasa Lila without anklets. Their dance, rooted in love and respect for each other and the land, impressed all the beings of all the realms.

High up in the heavens, the dance caught the eye of Ananta, the celestial snake on which Lord Vishnu reclined while floating in the cosmic ocean. Ananta carried all the known universes on his hood, along with all the precious gems to have ever existed. Ananta realized that he could not take his eyes off the divine couple as they danced, and the beauty of the land only enhanced the grace of the dance. Just as Krishna's Rasa Lila had moved Parvati to want to dance, Ananta was moved to honour the valley that Shiva had created for his dance.

Ananta took the biggest gem, the jewel in the centre of the crown, and presented it to the land itself.

This gem, known in Sanskrit as a *mani*, was embedded into the essence of the land, making it shine as brightly as the gem had. Before Lord Shiva drained the lake to create the valley, the mountains and forests around the lake had been the abode of forest deities called Umang Lai.

Inspired by the dance and the newly radiant land, Sidaba Mapa, the most powerful being from the mountains, understood that this was the right time to bring humans to the valley. Drawing from the essence of the divinity in the valley, the powers of the sun, and Umang Lai's own powers from the forest, Sidaba Mapa rubbed his hands together and created the first of the human beings to live in the valley. Like the gods and goddesses before them, the people, too, continued dancing the Rasa Lila, though it was now called Manipuri. Manipur was the new name of the land, which was illuminated by the sheer brilliance of the gem that once graced the hood of the king of serpents, Ananta. Manipur stands for the 'land of the gem' where *mani* means 'gem' and *pur* means 'land.'

KNOW YOUR STATES

- Manipur is also known as the Dragon State of India. Historically known as the Kangleipak kingdom, Manipur has a rich cultural tradition featuring dragon motifs and dragon worship.
- Imphal is the capital of Manipur. The name Imphal comes from the Manipuri language where it is also pronounced as 'Yum-phal.' In Manipuri, *yum* means 'house' and *phal* means 'beautiful or plenty.' The words when put together mean 'plenty of beautiful houses.'
- The official language of Manipur is Meitei, also known as Manipuri.
- Keibul Lamjao Floating Park in Manipur is said to be the world's only floating national park. It is home to the endangered Sangai or the brow-antlered deer.
- Manipur has the world's oldest polo ground at Imphal's Mapal Kangjeibung.

16

MEGHALAYA

The Land of the Clouds

High up in the mountains is a land so mystical and magical that you can reach up and touch the clouds that float so low that they gently graze your head. The land is so beautiful that it looks like it was blessed by the heavens many times over. There are towering trees, rolling green hills, and sparkling rivers where the gaze falls. And in the centre is a sacred mountain that rises so high up that its summit kisses the sky. The peak of this mountain is called U Lum Sohpetbneng, which translates to the 'navel of heaven' in the Khasi language. Just as the navel in the human body reminds humans of the link they once had with their mother when they were inside her womb, U Lum Sohpetbneng reminds the Khasi people of this land and how their ancestors descended from the clouds above.

Legend says that in the beginning, when the world had just begun and everything was brand new, this sacred peak was the site of a golden bridge called Jingkieng Ksiar, or a golden ladder. The golden ladder that shimmered with the colours of the rainbow and the splendour of the sun was built by U Blei Trai Kynrad – God, Creator, and Lord Master. The Lord Master lived in the heavens in the upper reaches of the clouds, where everything was peaceful and quiet, along with sixteen families who were the ancestors of the Khasi people.

The ancestors lived in nine huts in the clouds. However, as the land below was connected to them through the golden bridge, these ancestors made it a practice to go to the land below on earth, where they had seven huts set up for them for the day. The Lord Master had told the humans that they could use the golden ladder and go to earth as they pleased, but they had to go back to heaven for the night. Back then, the only living beings on earth were the various kinds of animals, birds, reptiles, and insects. There were also plants and trees of different varieties that provided food and shelter to these creatures. The humans would come down the golden ladder and spend the day marvelling at these beings and life forms that the Lord

Master had made. Life in the beginning was all about harmony. All of the Lord Master's creations spoke one language. The humans, the animals and birds, and even the plants and flowers were able to communicate with each other and lived harmoniously as one.

As time passed, the Creator taught the sixteen families in heaven how to cultivate crops and grow things of their own accord. The humans discovered that the soil around the sacred mountain U Lum Sohpetbneng was fertile and perfect to grow their own crops. So, the sixteen families tried their luck at planting their own fields and felt joy when they saw the seeds they had planted spring up as saplings.

However, despite the peace and harmony within the sixteen families, there was one who was not happy. Why did he have to go back to heaven every night? Why did he have to live peacefully with animals when he was a 'superior' human? Why couldn't he cut trees as he pleased? He was a human who lived in heaven with clouds and stars, yet he had no power of his own. Every single thing he had to do was based on what the Lord Master decreed. He was tired of listening to the Lord Master, and he wanted to control the rest of the humans himself. So, he waited for an opportunity to do just that.

One day, only seven families came down the golden bridge to work on their fields. The remaining nine stayed in heaven. The unsatisfied human knew that it would be easier to subdue these seven families and take over power, than if all of them were on earth together. He ran to the golden ladder with his axe and cut it down, severing the connection between heaven and earth. The seven families who were down on earth were now stranded here forever.

With the cutting of the golden bridge, great changes happened on earth. The one language that had once united them all splintered into many. Humans stopped understanding the language of plants and animals. The descendants of the evil one found more and more things to be unsatisfied by and lived their lives only to fulfil their selfish needs. However, not all was lost. The seven families who were stranded did their best to pass on all the wonderful lessons they had learnt from the Lord Master. They taught the people on earth lessons of peace, justice, and harmony. They taught them how to revere nature. They taught them how important it was to take care of the rivers, the mountains, and the earth. They told them to always remember the time when this land was the link between heaven and earth and how that sacred connection meant that it had to be protected at all costs. They hoped that the people after them would continue to uphold their sacred truth and nurture Mother Earth. The descendants of these families made sure to pass the story on through generations in the hope that the lessons would live on and that the people of today would choose to live as those seven families did, according to the will of the Lord Master.

Even today, the people of the land feast their eyes on the sacred peak U Leum Sohpetbneng and remember how their land was not just close to the clouds but a part of the literal clouds of heaven itself because of the golden ladder that rose up from this point. And so, it is little wonder that the state was named Meghalaya as *megha* means 'clouds' and *alaya* means 'the home of,' reminding all that Meghalaya not only was but continues to be the abode of clouds.

KNOW YOUR STATES

- Meghalaya is known as the Scotland of the East. It is said that the British colonial officers referred to Meghalaya this way as the rolling hills of the land reminded them of home.
- Meghalaya's capital city, Shillong, is named after Leishyllong, the supreme God who is said to live on a peak overlooking the city.
- The main languages spoken in Meghalaya are Khasi, Garo, and English.
- Laho is a famous dance form from Meghalaya. This is a vibrant dance performed by the people of the Pnar tribe.
- Mawsynram in Meghalaya holds the world record for the highest amount of rainfall received. Previously, Cherrapunji, known locally as Sohra, held the record for the wettest place on earth.
- Meghalaya is also famous for its living root bridges made by the Khasi people from the aerial roots of rubber fig trees.

17

MIZORAM

The Land of the Mizo People

The story of the name behind certain lands is knitted into the stories of their people. Mizoram is one such state. To know the story behind the name 'Mizoram,' one needs to know the story of its people. And that story begins many thousands of years ago with a creator goddess called Khuanu. Khuanu was the creator of all the human beings and all the animals. Upon creation, the humans and animals spoke to each other in one language. They lived together peacefully. They gathered food together. They shared the fruit up on the trees. Khuanu was happy to see how harmoniously all her creations lived. Khuanu loved each and every one of her creations just like a mother loves her children. As time passed, the people multiplied on earth, and they realized they needed someone to lead them. However, as they were created equal, they did not have a natural ruler between them, so they decided to select a chief for their tribe.

One day, the chief fell into a deep sleep, and he had a terrible dream. The chief dreamt that he had transformed into a ferocious creature called the Awk, swallowing the moon. He dreamt that because the moon was swallowed, a great darkness engulfed the land, leaving its inhabitants terrified of what was to follow. Later on in the dream, he saw the Awk spitting

the moon out again, restoring light to the land and its people. As soon as the moon was spat out, the dream ended, and the chief woke up. He gathered the tribe around and told them of his strange dream. Then he said that he could still feel the pain of eating the moon in his mouth. When the people who were standing nearby came to check, they were astonished to see blood trickling out from the chief's mouth.

A year later, the chief passed away, and then something unthinkable happened. He transformed into the Awk, just as he had in his dream. The Awk flew up to the moon. But the moon was so full that night that he was unable to swallow it. The Awk waited till the next day, when the moon would be smaller, and then he tried again. This time, the Awk was able to swallow the moon whole. The people of the land wanted to save the moon from the Awk. They decided to retaliate by making as much noise as possible. They grabbed any instrument or tool that they could and started to make loud noise. The Awk was horrified to hear the loud, deafening noise that the people made. Startled and confused, it spat the moon out. From then on, whenever the Awk swallowed the moon, the people would start banging on things and making a loud din to rescue the moon.

One day, however, the Awk decided to go after yet another target. This time, it decided to swallow the sun. Once the sun was completely inside the Awk's mouth, a great and terrible darkness enveloped the land. All the living beings on the land were terrified and they called the phenomenon Thim Zing or the Great Dark. They were not able to see anything and were scared of living in utter darkness. And with good reason, for every inanimate object sprang back to life. Wood that had been cut and kept aside to build fires for warmth and cooking became green again. The only things that remained in their inanimate form were the skulls of animals once hunted for food by the great warriors known as the Pasaltha. The Pasaltha tried to use the skulls to burn fires that would bring light and warmth to their people and let them cook some food. But the fires would not burn for long.

As the great darkness continued, people could neither stay warm nor feed themselves, and they started transforming into animals of all sorts. The ones who were to work the fields became laughing thrushes. The people who went fishing for crabs in boats on the rivers while holding torches became fireflies. The men and women who wore traditional striped clothes and turbans became tigers. The women who worked with dyes to colour their fabrics became gibbons whose palms were dark in colour. Some of the transformations were based on the tribe the people belonged to. Some tribes transformed into all kinds of squirrels. Some tribes turned into elephants. Some even became monkeys. On and on, the transformations continued till, at last, the whole world was almost entirely animals, birds, insects, and plants.

Goddess Khuanu, who had been watching all of this unfold, could not bear to witness her creations suffer any longer. She knew that she had to save them in whichever way she could. Before all of the people were transformed forever, the goddess took a couple of people from each tribe of humans and placed them in a deep pit in the ground. Then, she sealed the entrance to the pit with a massive rock called Chhinlung. In the Mizo language, *Chhinlung* means 'enclosed with a rock.' These humans who had been saved from being transformed into animals waited quietly in the pit for the time of the terrible darkness to end.

One day, after the Great Dark had ended and life had returned to normal, the goddess decided that it was safe for the humans that she had saved to come back out again. Goddess Khuanu moved the rock that she had used to seal the pit. Out came all the different clans of the Mizo people, ready to repopulate their land. This is called *Chhinlung Chhuak* in Mizo, which means 'coming out from the earth.' The Mizo people who emerged out of the darkness were ready to live in harmony with the animals and nature. The legend of their origins is a testament to their resilience and warrior spirit. They had survived the darkest of times and emerged into the light to tell their tale, the tale of the Mizo people. The name Mizoram means the 'land of the Mizo people.'

KNOW YOUR STATES

- Mizoram is also known as the land of the Highlanders. As you read in the story, the meaning of the name of the state is also the land of the Mizos, people who lived in the highlands or the hills.
- The religion of the ancient Mizo people was called Sakhua, and it is still practised in Mizoram today.
- Aizawl is the capital of Mizoram. The word Aizawl is a combination of two Mizo words – *Ai* means 'cardamom' and *zawl* means 'flatland' or 'plain.' Put together, the name means a 'field of wild cardamom.'
- The official language of Mizoram is Mizo.
- One of the oldest dance forms from Mizoram is the Cheraw dance, also known as the bamboo dance.
- Mizoram's traditional dress includes the Puan, a beautifully handwoven wraparound skirt worn mainly by women. Women pair it with a blouse, while men wear traditional cloth wraps called sayn around their waists.

18

NAGALAND

The Land of the Nagas

The people of Nagaland, known as Nagas, believe that their their origins trace back to the creation of their land by a powerful, shape-shifting, creator deity whom they call Lijaba. Lijaba was the one who created the sun and the moon. And according to Naga legends, it was Lijaba who created the world.

Have you noticed how most of us tend to start projects with a lot of planning and care? Well, Lijaba was no different. When he started with his work of putting the world together, he decided to pay a lot of attention to detail. He began by making valleys that were broad and even. He created plains that were so level that one could use a ruler and see how flat and straight they were. On and on he went, so immersed in his work that he forgot that where there are forces of creation, there are always forces of destruction ready to tear down what has been built. He worked on steadily till there was only a little bit left to complete.

Lijaba had just started working on the final part, which was the beautiful land that would become Nagaland, when a giant cockroach appeared. According to Naga legend, giant cockroaches were ancient beings who had been around since the beginning of time. Now, one of these had decided to come to Lijaba to tell him that there were evil forces who did not want this world to be built. The evil forces knew that if they could stop Lijaba before he completed his work then this world would never be built. So, they needed to stop him midway. The giant cockroach urged Lijaba to speed up and complete his creation of the world. There was no time to waste on levelling things and making sure that everything was even and steady. Time was running out, they had to build and create swiftly, before everything was lost forever

At the giant cockroach's warning, Lijaba leapt into action at full speed. He quickly shaped hills and valleys. He did not wait to smooth them out or level the land's features. And then Lijaba moved on to the work of creating the protectors of the land.

High up on one of the hills Lijaba had created, he set up six stones from where three men and three women would emerge. These people would be the protectors of the land and the people from whom all mankind would emerge. These six early humans would belong to different clans. With his work thus done, Lijaba retreated to the heavens, happy that he had completed his work before the evil forces had attacked him. Now that the evil forces had been thwarted, humanity could finally emerge.

After the last bit of land that Lijaba had created settled into its grooves and stood steady, the humans started emerging from behind the rocks that Lijaba had established. According to Naga mythology, a pair with a man and woman each, brother and sister, in fact, appeared from three different clans called Pongen, Jami, and Longkum. The three men and three women paired up by choosing a partner from a clan that was not their own. Then they went in different directions to establish villages and tribes of their own.

These first humans were closest to the god who had created them. So, like Lijaba, they, too, could communicate with species that were not their own. They could speak to plants and animals, and could do things that many humans today cannot dream of. Each tribe of humans that was created formed special bonds with certain animals. Some who loved elephants went to the south of the land they lived in. Some of those who found the habitat of camels more to their liking went to the deserts of the world. And then there were those who communicated with snakes and water serpents. Legend says that over time these humans established a kingdom underwater, with capital cities in the depths of rivers.

The ancient word for snakes was 'nagas,' and it was these reptile nagas who protected the rivers, forests, and natural treasures of the world. They were said to have the ability to control the rains. Some myths said that it was these naga guardians who decided which parts of land could be used for agriculture and

which could not. The humans who communicated with and lived with these snakes and serpents took up their ways. They lived in the forest and around the rivers. Like the snakes and serpents, they, too, were serious about protecting the natural world that was their home.

As time passed, the humans who loved the nagas and thought of them as their totem and inspiration began to be known as Nagas themselves. The Nagas were known all over the Indian subcontinent as fierce people who loved their land and the animals in it with a touching ferocity. As legend tells it, the people who lived in that last bit of land that Lijaba created with such great haste were the descendants of these original Nagas. Known for their warrior skill and their love for the land, the land itself came to be known by their name, and that is the name we all know it by today – the 'land of the Nagas' or Nagaland.

KNOW YOUR STATES

- Nagaland is also called the Falcon Capital of the World. More than a million Amur falcons roost in Nagaland during their annual migration, attracting ornithologists and scientists to come study the birds.
- Nagaland's capital, Kohima, got its name from *Kewhima*, which in the local language means 'the place where the Kewhi flower grows.'
- Though English is the official language of Nagaland, the most spoken language is Nagamese.
- The state animal of Nagaland is the Mithun or the drung ox, a kind of domestic cattle that is found only in that region.
- The most famous festival in the state is the Hornbill Festival that celebrates the spirit and songs of the Naga tribe.
- Nagaland is known for its exquisite handwoven fabrics, bamboo crafts, and wood carvings.

19

ODISHA

The Land of the Odras

Odisha is a land of many legends and myths, each one different from the other as it is also a land of many tribes and indigenous people. This particular story comes from the Khond tribe, which is Odisha's largest and one of the oldest tribes. The Khonds are hunter-gatherers, and they are known for their rich cultural heritage. As told in the stories of the Khond people, Odisha and its people came to be because that was what their Sun God wanted.

Now, in the beginning there was only the Sun God who was called Bura Penu. Alone in the vast emptiness, Bura Penu grew a bit bored. So, he created Tanapenu, the Earth God. Bura Penu was not really looking for company, though, he was looking for someone who could serve him. Bura Penu set Tanapenu to work, but as things turned out, Tanapenu did not make

Bura Penu happy. It was time to create something else. And that is how Bura Penu decided to make some human beings.

Being the Sun God, all Bura Penu had to do was throw a fistful of soil in a certain direction to create humans and they would be made. But Tanapenu did not want Bura Penu to create humans. So, he waited for Bura Penu to pick up some soil and throw it behind his shoulder. As soon as the soil hit the ground, Tanapenu picked it up and threw it in another direction. The soil hit the ground and out sprang some plants and vegetation. Suddenly, the land blossomed with plants – bamboo, teak, rosewood, sal, and many more.

Bura Penu waited for a while for the humans, but none were to be found. He decided to try again. He took a second fistful of soil and threw it behind him. Once again, Tanapenu immediately picked it up and threw it in another direction. This time, the soil fell in water and out sprang all the aquatic animals that the world has ever seen. The waters of the land started teeming with catfish, prawns, ribbonfish, and pomfret. The neighbouring seas filled with turtles and dolphins. Bura Penu was puzzled. This was not what he had expected. He waited, and then with no humans in sight, wondered why no humans had emerged.

But he would not give up. Bura Penu took up a third fistful of soil and threw it behind him again. You already know what happened next, Tanapenu jumped right on it. He threw the soil in another direction, and this time, out came all the land animals that the world has ever seen. Tigers, lions, crocodiles, deer, antelope, gaurs, langurs, and pangolins ambled, galloped, trotted, and walked onto the land. On and on and on went the wondrous collection of animals that would now call this land home.

Bura Penu sighed. He appreciated all the new creations that had emerged. But why was making humans so hard? He would not give up though. He took a fourth fistful of soil and threw it behind him. And as Tanapenu had been doing all this while, he took the soil and threw it off in another direction, creating all the creatures that fly. Bulbuls and hornbills. Crows and cuckoos. Koels and kingfishers. Cawing and cooing, whistling and warbling – the birds of many feathers flapped their wings and filled the skies. This time, though, Bura Penu had turned around to see why the humans had not been created yet and he saw what Tanapenu had been doing. Bura Penu crinkled his eyes and furrowed his brow and shook his fist!

'Aha! I see you, you sneaky Tanapenu! This is why I've not been able to make any humans! Now I know what you have been up to!' he yelled at him.

Angry at being tricked, Bura Penu grabbed a large fistful of soil and threw it directly at the back of Tanapenu, the Earth God. And finally, now that the soil had been thrown in the correct direction and because it had touched the Earth God, out sprang the first humans. Then Bura Penu scraped some of the dirt off his palm and blew it in all the directions of the world creating love, compassion, goodwill, and all those good things that people needed to live a happy life in their land. The story goes that this is how the first people came to live in this land.

The language that the people of the land spoke was called Odra Prakrit. Despite all the differences between the people who lived across the land, the language was what united them. As the people set up villages, towns, and kingdoms in the area, the word *odra* was used to indicate to outsiders that this was the language of the place. The land where the people spoke Odra came to be so famous that it was even mentioned in the ancient Indian epic the Mahabharata. The land became home to famous kingdoms and iconic kings like Ashoka, who adopted non-violence and spread the teachings of Gautama Buddha to lands far and wide. The land was called Odra Desha, or the land where Odra was spoken. Odra Desha became Uddisa.

As centuries passed, the language came to be known as Odia, and then Oriya. In modern times, the land of Odra Desha or Uddisa came to be known as Orissa for a very long time. But the thing about stories of yore is that they can be forgotten for a while but not completely erased. So, the people of this land where Odra was spoken, this land that was known as Odra Desha, asked for the name of the land to reflect its roots. And that is how it came to be known as Odisha, as we know it today.

KNOW YOUR STATES

- Odisha is also called the Soul of India. The state is known for its rich cultural heritage, breathtaking natural beauty, and unique tourist attractions.
- Odisha was formerly known as Orissa from 1950 to 2011.
- Bhubaneshwar is the capital of Odisha. The city is said to derive its name from Tribhubaneshawar, which means 'the Lord of all three worlds.' This is a reference to Lord Shiva who is considered the main deity of the region.
- The official language of Odisha is Odia.
- The most famous classical dance of Odisha is Odissi.
- The state is known for its unique handicrafts, such as Pattachitra paintings and silver filigree work.
- Odisha was also known as the kingdom of Kalinga.
- The thirteenth-century Sun Temple of Konark is one of Odisha's most famous monuments. It was designated a UNESCO world heritage site in 1984.

20

PUNJAB

The Land of Five Rivers

Many millennia ago, at the meeting point of five ancient rivers named Vipasa, Satadru, Iravati, Chandrabhaga, and Vitasta was an ancient kingdom called Pancanada. This kingdom was said to be blessed by mystical powers. Deep under the waters of these rivers lived a demon king called Jalandara, who longed to conquer all three realms – the heavens, the earth, and the underworld. According to a legend in an ancient Indian text called the Skanda Purana, Jalandara himself was born from rage. The story goes that the king of gods, Lord Indra, had tried to attack Lord Shiva, the destroyer, with his thunderbolt. Enraged, Lord Shiva had opened his third eye to focus on Indra and burn him to the ground. However, Indra managed to dodge Lord Shiva's fiery beam of anger.

The anger thus released had to go somewhere, so Lord Shiva poured his anger out into the ocean.

The ocean welcomed Shiva's rage and shaped it into a little boy named Jalandara, where *jal* means 'water' and *andar* means 'within.' As a little boy, Jalandara cried a lot trying to find out where he came from. He cried so loud and so often that the earth itself shook in response. The god of the ocean Samudra tried his best to calm him down. He used ocean currents to help him fly over the waves. He sent him out to the shore to hunt and be merry. He gave him power over all the largest fish in the waters and the birds in the sky. Yet, born out of rage, Jalandara could never find peace no matter what he did.

Jalandara was trained in the art of war and on how to be a king by Shukra, the guru of the *asura*s (demons). When Jalandara grew up, he got married to a wise and lovely asura princess called Vrinda, who helped him be as happy as he could be despite all the anger he felt inside. With Vrinda by his side, his training in weapons, and his own talents, Jalandara became the emperor of the asuras. As he had grown up underwater, he built his kingdom in the water as well, with his capital city at the point where the five rivers met, Pancanada.

As Jalandara was born from the anger of one of the most powerful gods, he had the divine ability to control fire and water, and he could move things with his mind.

Jalandara was a just and noble king, and his subjects loved him. But Jalandara felt a constant yearning for something in his soul. He ended up

starting battles with the gods. Jalandara won every battle that he fought against the gods, ultimately becoming the lord of the three worlds – the heavens, the earth, and the underworld. To celebrate his victory, Jalandara took over all the jewels that the gods and other celestial beings had ever collected, making his kingdom the wealthiest that had ever existed. He even captured gods and made them live under his rule in his kingdom.

The gods were upset at the loss of their power and dignity. They wanted to defeat Jalandara once and for all. So, they decided to send Narada, the messenger of the gods, to Jalandara to provoke him. Jalandara welcomed Narada with great warmth and gave him a tour of his kingdom. Narada took it all in and then said that it did not compare to Lord Shiva's own kingdom, Kailash. Jalandara was enraged at Narada's words. He now wished to own all that Lord Shiva did. He challenged Lord Shiva to come fight him in the battlefield if he dared. Lord Shiva was furious at the challenge and went and met the demon king. Thus, the battle began.

Jalandara was trained in many kinds of martial arts. He was also an expert in the art of illusion. Jalandara kept tricking the forces of Lord Shiva. His vast army of trained demons also fought valiantly. Jalandara met each and every one of the generals of Lord Shiva and vanquished them all. Finally, after many weeks of intense battle, it was time for Lord Shiva and Jalandara to come face to face. As they battled each other, both the god whose rage had created this demon of rage and the demon king himself knew that they would not show the opponent any mercy.

Just before they started to fight, Jalandara looked around him. Most of his army lay defeated on the battleground, weak and helpless. Some of them had fled. It was now up to him. Jalandara knew that he did not want to fight any longer, but he also would not be the one who walked away. Lord Shiva knew that it was time for this powerful demon's story to end. Lord Shiva brought out the Chakra, a divine weapon that was created from his toe, and with a swift motion he used it on Jalandara and ended his story. The rage that had filled the asura emptied out and flowed back into Lord Shiva's third eye. God closed his third eye again and blessed the land where Jalandara had lived and ruled to always be home to strong warriors who believed in themselves and their people. Lord Shiva also deemed that no natural calamity would ever befall this land.

As the story goes, the city that Jalandara ruled from in ancient times is the modern city of Jalandhar in the state of Punjab. And that Punjab itself is the kingdom called Pancanada that is mentioned in the ancient story. The five rivers that flow through Punjab are the Beas, Sutlej, Ravi, Chenab and Jhelum. The people of Punjab are called Punjabis, and their language is also known as Punjabi. In Punjabi, the word *punj* means 'five' and the word *aab* means 'any body of water.' When you put it all together, the word Punjab means the 'land of five waters' or the 'land of the five rivers.'

KNOW YOUR STATES

- Punjab is also called the Bread Basket of India. The state is known for its rich soil, excellent farming techniques, and high food grain production.
- The capital city of Punjab is Chandigarh.
- Punjabi is the main language spoken in the state and is written in the Gurmukhi script.
- The most famous dance form from Punjab is the vibrant and exuberant dance form of Bhangra.
- The state is well known for the Golden Temple, a site of great significance for Sikhs.
- Makki Di Roti (roti made from cornmeal) and Sarson Ka Saag (spicy mustard greens) is a famous dish in the region.
- Punjab is home to the Wagah border that has a ceremonial border crossing between India and Pakistan.
- Punjab celebrates festivals like Lohri, Baisakhi, and Gurpurab with great enthusiasm

21

RAJASTHAN

The Land of the Rajputs

The legend of the land known as the land of the Rajputs begins at a time when the greatest warriors had been vanquished and erased. Without the good to defend the land, evil had lifted its head up again. Convinced that there was no one to stop them from running amok over the land, evil spread over the land in the form of demons known as *asuras* and *danavas*. The wise men and women of the land decided it was time to do something. They all got together and asked the holy men Agastya, Gautama, Vasishta, and Vishwamitra to help create a new race of warriors. They were considered the best people for the job as they were wise teachers who understood the mysteries of life, and could communicate with gods and goddesses even though they themselves were human.

The sages gathered all the good and learned people they could and set up space for a huge ritual or a puja at Sage Vasishta's hermitage or ashram. Vasishta's ashram was deep in the middle of the Arbudaranya forest, high on top of a mountain by the same name. Mount Arbudaranya was a sacred place, and it was also said to be the home of a holy serpent called Arbuda who had saved the life of Lord Shiva's sacrificial bull, Nandi. The sages knew that it was the perfect location to start creating a new set of warriors who would protect the earth from the evil that had arisen on it.

The first step to performing this puja was to build a massive pit that would act as an altar to house a gigantic fire with flames that would touch the heavens. As the sages started building the altar, the asuras who lived in the forest came to know of what was happening. They immediately rushed to the ashram, determined to put an end to the proceedings.

Each time the sages took a few steps ahead to proceed with the rituals, the asuras would interrupt the process. Sometimes they rushed at the fire with bags of garbage and threw it around the area, forcing the sages to stop and clean up before they could continue with the rites and rituals. Sometimes the asuras would prance into the area, interrupting the sages as they were in the middle of chanting, making them begin again and again, till the sun went down and it was too late to continue with the puja.

The great Sage Vasishta had enough of their antics, and he decided to do yet another puja. At the break of dawn, he secretly built a massive fire pit and meditated

and prayed to all the gods and goddesses, till out stepped a great warrior by the name of Pratihara, one of the first Rajputs to have been created from fire itself. Pratihara was unequalled in the art of protection. Nothing got by his watch. The sage Vasishta placed him in charge of protecting the paths to the hermitage.

As Vasishta meditated on Agni, the god of fire, to create Pratihara, some of the sages were busy meditating on Brahma, the god of creation, to help them with the creation of a warrior who would fend off the asuras. Brahma heard their prayers and then created a hero from the water of the Ganges that was in his folded palm. In Sanskrit, the word for folded palm was *chuluka*, and so the hero was named Chulukya so that people would always know where he originated from.

There was yet another group of sages that was also conducting a ritual like this away from the eyes of the asuras and the danavas. To their delight, their sacrificial fire produced a warrior who stepped out wearing a crown and golden armour and holding a bow. This warrior who had the fiercest expression on his face was named Paramara or the slayer of enemies.

The three heroes immediately banded together and formed a protective zone where the sages could continue with their rituals. As the heroes fought valiantly, Sage Vasishta continued with the rituals that the asuras and danavas had interrupted. As the flames blazed high, with the smoke reaching the heavens, a four-armed warrior stepped out of the flames. In each of his four hands he held a sword, a shield, a bow, and an arrow. Vasishta named him Chauhvana and commanded him to protect the hermitage and the land from all evil. Chauhvana accepted his orders and went ahead and joined the other three who were already fighting.

The warriors were strong and undefeatable, but the sages knew that they would need more to defeat the strongest of the demons. As if in response to their thoughts, Goddess Ashapura appeared in front of them. The magnificent goddess had seven pairs of eyes that took in all the sights in front of her. She glowed with the strength of her powers. The learned men and women bowed in front of her, overjoyed that the goddess had taken their side. For Goddess Ashapura was named after her ability to fulfil the wishes of all those who prayed to her. She blessed the warriors with infinite strength and endurance. She promised the sages that she would stand by the warriors for all eternity. Empowered by the goddess's presence, the warriors felt as if their strength was doubling. They started taking down the demons one by one. The last ones to fall were the demons Yantraketu and Dhoomaketu, who crumpled and transformed into a million asteroids in the night sky, which was the domain of Chandra, the moon god. The demons would never be able to torment the people of earth again.

The warriors had fought with grace and dignity, empowered by the powers of Agni, Brahma, and Ashapura. The warriors went on to create tribes and kingdoms of their own and became kings who were known for their bravery, courage, and loyalty. The descendants of these warriors were known as Rajputs, the word meaning 'the sons of kings.' As time passed, Mount Arbudaranya, where the hermitage of Sage Vasishta was, came to be known as Mount Abu. The land where the Rajputs lived and established kingdoms came to be known as Rajputana. When India gained independence, all the warrior kingdoms came together and the name was changed to Rajasthan, which still reminds us of the warrior kings and queens that gave this land its rich culture and heritage.

KNOW YOUR STATES

- Rajasthan is also known as the Land of Kings due to its history of powerful royal kingdoms.
- Jaipur is the capital of Rajasthan. Jaipur gets its name from its founder Maharaja Jai Singh, who was also a great warrior and an astronomer.
- The main language spoken in Rajasthan is Rajasthani.
- Rajasthan is India's largest state in terms of geographical area.
- The majority of the Thar Desert, also known as the Great Indian Desert, is in Rajasthan. According to some local folklore and versions of the Ramayana, Lord Ram is believed to have created the desert.
- Rajasthan has eight UNESCO World Heritage Sites, which includes monuments like Chittorgarh Fort, Kumbhalgarh Fort, Ranthambore Fort, Gagron Fort, Amber Fort, Jaisalmer Fort, Jantar Mantar, and Keoladeo National Park.
- Rajasthan is known for festivals like the Pushkar Fair and the International Camel Festival.

22

SIKKIM

The Land of the New Palace

High up in the mountains, protected from curious eyes and the occasional wanderer, the king of gods Indra ruled over a city. A city that was so beautiful that it was filled with rivers of nectar, incredibly lush gardens, and skies filled with divine light. Indra invited gods and goddesses to use it as a gateway point from heaven to earth and earth to heaven. He named his city Indrakil, or the walled city of Indra. Tales of this mythical city abounded through the three realms of heaven, earth, and the underworld. Beings from many realms travelled to Indrakil, only to settle down there and call it their home. And then there were the deities who had always called this land home.

Chief among them was the supreme creator called Itbu Rum. Itbu Rum had not just made the land. He was also part of the land. He had created the mountains, the rivers, the forests, and the animals. He had created the sacred mountain Kanchenjunga that Indrakil was on. The name Kanchenjunga meant 'the five treasures of snow,' each treasure standing for one of the five peaks of this mountain. Each peak was said to contain gold, silver, grains, gems, and sacred religious texts.

Mount Kanchenjunga was to be the eternal guardian of the land around it. It would stand tall forever, watching over the people who would live in its shadow. The peak of this mighty mountain would be the first to be touched by the rising sun's rays every morning, and the one to be bid goodbye by the last rays as the sun set every evening. Itbu Rum was the one who created the Lepcha people, a tribe that lives in the north-eastern mountains of India. It was the Lepchas who would be entrusted with taking care of this land with its mountains and rivers. The creator god gathered up the pure snow that enveloped the peaks of Mount Kanchenjunga and created a man called Fodongthing and a woman called Nazongnyu. Then Itbu Rum blessed these people with the knowledge of the beautiful, intricate connection between humanity and nature. He told them that they were god's favourite children who were created here in what he called Mayel Lyang or a land of eternal bliss.

The word Lepcha meant 'the beloved children of the snowy ranges.' Itbu Rum told the first Lepcha man and first Lepcha woman to marry, start a family, and settle on the land to care for it. Itbu Rum also gave the Lepcha people a script to communicate and document the ways in which they lived, so that the Lepcha way of living would always live on.

Blessed by having originated from the pure snow of what could only be described as paradise, the Lepcha tribe grew and grew under the watchful eye of Mount Kanchenjunga. The land they lived in was known for the value they placed in the sacred bond between humans and nature. They protected the land by keeping strict rules against overhunting and cutting down sacred trees, and protecting streams against pollution. In their language, the Lepcha started to call the land Nye-mae-el, meaning 'paradise.'

As the Lepcha tribe grew, the land came to be ruled by kings who believed this land protected by the sacred Kanchenjunga was indeed paradise on earth. These kings called the land 'Bayul' or a hidden paradise on earth. And as this was a divine land, the rulers who called themselves the Chogyals considered themselves the divine protectors of the land. These monarchs vowed to never summit or climb Mount Kanchenjunga as it would be disrespectful to step on the very mountains that were the reason why they were created. They believed that Mount Kanchenjunga was not only home to Itbu Rum and other gods and goddesses, but also other powerful spirits and deities that would protect

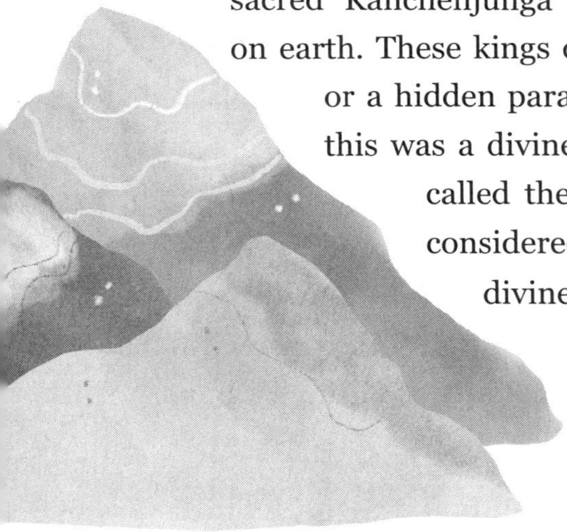

their kingdom. The Chogyal monarchs had elaborate rituals and festivals honouring all the mountain spirits that shielded their kingdom from avalanches, floods, and other natural disasters.

One of the most famous of the Chogyal kings was a monarch by the name of Tensung Namgyal. His coronation took place in a city called Yuksom, but Tensung Namgyal wanted to move the capital city to another place. The place he chose was a region called Rabdentse, where he built a magnificent palace that boasted of amazing views of Mount Kanchenjunga and other mountains that were part of the same range. Tensung Namgyal was an enterprising king who wanted to expand the land. He did so by marrying princesses from distant lands. Tensung Namgyal had queens whom he had married from the kingdoms of Bhutan and Tibet.

After the palace was ready in his new capital city of Rabdentse, Tensung Namgyal married for the third time. This time, he married a princess from a tribe called the Limbu tribe from the Arun valley. The Limbu princess was called Thungwamukma. The king brought his new Limbu Queen Thungwamukma home and gave her a grand tour of the palace. He gave her the special honour of naming it. The queen thought for a bit and pronounced the new name of the palace in her own Limbu language. The new name that Queen Thungwamukma came up with was Song-Khyim. When asked to translate, the queen replied that she had named the palace 'New palace.' The word *song* meant 'new' and *khyim* meant 'palace' or 'home.' The people cheered at her reply even though it meant that she had given the 'new palace' the name 'New Palace' in her own language.

As time passed, Queen Thungwamukma's new name for her new home became the name for a land that was known by many names before. From Indrakil to Mayel Lyang to Nyae-mae-el to Bayal to Song-Khyim to finally just Sukhim. The word entered the language of the people and was used forever more to refer to the kingdom that grew in the shadow of the powerful Mount Kanchenjunga in the north-eastern part of India. As time passed, Sukhim gave way to the name that we now know it by – Sikkim, one of the seven states of the northeast region of India.

KNOW YOUR STATES

- Sikkim is also known as the Valley of Rice. The state is famous for its fertile lands that are perfect to cultivate rice and for its large-scale rice production.
- Sikkim is home to the third-highest peak in the world, Kanchenjunga, which is not just a mountain for the people of Sikkim but also a deity as we have seen in this story.
- Gangtok is the capital of Sikkim. The name Gangtok is derived from the Sikkimese words *gang*, which means 'hill,' and *tok*, which means 'cut.' Gangtok together is said to refer to the scenic way in which this capital is carved into the hillside, from where one can enjoy spectacular views of the Kanchenjunga.
- Sikkim has four official languages: Nepali, Sikkimese, Lepcha, and English.
- Some of the famous festivals of Sikkim are Sonam Lochar and Losar.
- Sikkim is the least populated state in India.
- Sikkim is well-known for the Ghantu dance performed by the Gurung community.
- A special variety of chilli called Dalle Khorsani grows in Sikkim. It is one of the hottest chillies in the world.

23

TAMIL NADU

The Land of the Tamils

There are many myths and legends about the land that is known as the country of the Tamils or the people who speak Tamil. This story takes you to the beginning of the universe as we know it, before the first unit of time had ever rung out. In the beginning, there was nothing but a deep, dark void. Lord Shiva, known as the destroyer, stood ready to bring an end to the great silence around him. Through destruction, he would begin creation – giving rise to countless universes and worlds. Lord Shiva assumed the role of Nataraja or the ultimate lord of dance. As Nataraja, it was the responsibility of Lord Shiva to take on the role of a cosmic dancer and bring about the creation of the world.

As he got ready to create the world, Nataraja held up all four of his hands. In one hand, he held a flame that would destroy darkness and illuminate the path forward. With another hand, he pointed towards his raised foot to indicate that he would always act as shelter for those in need. With his third hand, he blessed creation with all his might. And in the fourth one, he held his *damru*, the drum that would aid in all creation. Nataraja held the drum and shook it back and forth, and the silence of the deep, black void that was the only thing to have existed till then was destroyed by the sound that broke forth from the damru. The sound called 'Naadu' reverberated and shook the very atoms of the universe creating the universe as we now know it.

As the universe settled in and the planets and different realms, beings and creatures emerged, the sound from the damru echoed through the lands, creating the first languages known to man. From one side of the damru came Sanskrit. And from the other? Well, legend says that the other language, one of the first ever spoken by humans was Tamizh. Tamizh, or Tamil as the language was later known, was so beautiful that it transformed into a mother goddess called Tamil Thaayi or Mother Tamil. Tamil Thaayi was one of the most beautiful goddesses to have ever existed. She was goddess, mother, and maiden all in one. Tamil Thaayi had a bejewelled crown and dressed like a queen of the highest order. When she walked, she was enveloped in a golden hue that only added to her splendour. Tamil Thaayi considered the spread of Tamil as her own personal responsibility. In her four arms, she carried all the things she needed to pass the glorious language on to her believers. With two of her hands, she carried the Yazh, an ancient stringed musical instrument,

and in another she held a book written in Tamil. In her fourth hand, she held a baton that held out as she marched onward singing songs in Tamil and telling people about the importance of learning and speaking a classical language like Tamil.

Tamil Thaayi was much loved by the people who adopted the language that she stood for. They made pilgrimages to the Pottiyam mountains where she lived. They caught glimpses of her near the Vaigai River that she loved. Tamil Thaayi considered works written in Tamil literature to be gems and that is what her believers gifted her. Sage Agastya visited her at her abode in the mountains to gift her the Agattiyam, an ancient text that he wrote in Tamil to explain the grammar of the language. Tamil Thaayi accepted the work from him in joy, turning the book into a gem that adorned her crown, the moment her divine fingers touched it.

As Tamil Thaayi cast her blessings around, more and more royal families craved her presence in their courts. The kings and queens of the Pandya, Chera, and Chola dynasties invited her to their kingdoms. Their lands became Tamil-speaking lands. Famous poems and stories composed by Tamil poets adorned her as headpieces, earring, necklaces, bangles, waist ornaments, anklets, and more. While there were goddesses of learning and language in many countries around the world, it was only here that a language was the goddess herself.

Even after Tamil Thaayi stopped appearing physically in front of her people, the people who spoke her Tamil felt her presence in their life forever. The Tamil people loved their language like a child loved their mother. They felt the warm embrace of their language around them at all times. They believed that it was Tamil who gave birth to them and Tamil who raised them. Tamil put them to sleep at night with the gentlest of lullabies. Tamil taught them the first words that they spoke, lighting up the eyes of their mothers and fathers with pride and joy. Tamil was like the first milk that touched their tongues and like the first morsels of food that nourished them. Tamil was the language of their ancestors, and the people swore that it would be the language of their descendants. Tamil was the language of their home. And Tamil would be the language of their land as well.

As time passed, the Tamil people came to be known as Tamilians. The ancient country that was inhabited by the people who fervently believed in Goddess Tamil Thaayi and the language was known as Tamilakam. The word Tamilakam can be roughly translated as the 'home of the Tamil.' Later on, parts of Tamilakam were divided into regions called Perunadu, where *peru* means 'great' and *nadu* means 'country.' Tamilakam ended up being divided into thirteen nadus and they all spoke their own version of Tamil.

The Tamil people were empire builders, master craftsmen, and creators of art and literature. As their fame and influence grew, the language also spread from beyond the borders of Tamilakam to other parts of the world where Tamil started to be spoken as well. And so, the story goes that Tamilakam eventually came to be known as Tamil Nadu to mark its place in the world as the original land of the Tamil people.

KNOW YOUR STATES

- Tamil Nadu is also known as the Land of Temples. Tamil Nadu has more than thirty thousand temples that reflect the artistic and architectural styles of the dynasties that have ruled it over the ages.
- Ancient Tamil poets wrote about a lost continent called Kumarikkandam, which was supposed to be the cradle of a civilization that spoke only Tamil.
- Chennai is the capital of Tamil Nadu. The name Chennai comes from a famous general called Chennappa Nayaka, who first leased the land to the British. The British named the region Chennapattanam or the town of Chenna after this general. Chennapattanam was later shortened to Chennai.
- Bharatanatyam, the renowned classical dance form, originated in Tamil Nadu.
- Tamil Nadu celebrates vibrant festivals like Pongal, a harvest festival, and Thaipusam.
- The state animal of Tamil Nadu is the Nilgiri Tahr or the Nilgiri Ibex that is indigenous to the region.

24

TELANGANA

The Land with Three Shiva Lingams

This is a story of three episodes that feature gods, princesses, cowherds, and sheer belief. Three stories that are then linked together to become one that will tell us why the state of Telangana is called by that particular name.

We start with the mythical story of a demon called Tarakasura. Tarakasura, like many asuras before him, dreamt of taking over the heavens and ruling over the gods. To achieve his goal, Tarakasura meditated on Brahma for a very, very long time. When Brahma appeared in front of him, the asura asked him for two boons. One was that no one could be deemed his equal in all three worlds, and the second that only a son of Shiva could ever vanquish him in battle. Brahma granted him his boons, a decision that led to immediate consequences. Tarakasura immediately made his way to the heavens, threw out all the gods and established himself as their ruler.

Indra, the king of gods who had lost his throne, made his way to Brahma and asked him for his assistance. However, he was told that there was nothing that they could do but wait till Shiva's son, Karthikeya, was born. He was the only one who could vanquish this demon. Brahma's words eventually came true. Karthikeya was born and he rose quickly to become the commander of the gods. As had been predicted, it was his fate to battle this terrible demon who had humiliated the gods and threatened the fate of Karthikeya's father, Lord Shiva himself.

Karthikeya vanquished the demon in a terrible battle that lasted many days and many nights. Even though Tarakasura wanted to rule over the gods, he was also an ardent believer of Lord Shiva and was believed to have a Shiva Linga within him, giving him power from inside. When Karthikeya defeated the asura, legend goes that the Shiva Linga inside Tarakasura broke, and a piece fell on the land known as Draksharamam. A land that we will come back to later in this three-part story.

The second story in the series is that of Princess Chandravathi. Princess Chandravathi ruled a small kingdom near the forests of Nallamala. The princess was an ardent devotee of Lord Shiva. While the princess was a good ruler, she felt as if her calling was to a simpler life. So, one day, Princess Chandravathi gave up the throne, left her life as a royal princess, and

decided to lead a life in the forests. The princess built a small hut on a hill known as the Srisailam hill. She got a herd of cows and decided to lead her life there, taking care of the cows and spending the rest of her time meditating on Lord Shiva.

The princess found peace in this new life of hers. Before long, she noticed something unusual. A group of cows from her herd would disappear in the evening and reappear in the morning completely milked. Curious, the princess followed the cows one night, only to see them offer their milk up to a Shiva Linga in the middle of the forest. Amazed by the sight, the princess decided to build a shrine in the forest to this Shiva Linga that had spontaneously arisen on its own, proving how sacred this place where she had chosen to live was. In time, the princess's shrine became a famous temple that welcomed believers from far and wide. The Srisailam hills were also famously believed to be the home of Lord Shiva and Parvati. According to myth, Shiva and Parvati were said to have moved here to be closer to their son Karthikeya, who also lived in the southern part of the subcontinent. So maybe it was no surprise that Princess Chandravathi had found a mysterious Shiva Linga in the forests here!

And now for the third story, a simple story of a land called Kaleeshwaram that was home to two Shiva Lingas on a single pedestal. Legend goes that the first Linga appeared when River Godavari, that flows through the land, meditated on Lord Shiva. Shortly after that anyone who took a dip in the river seemed to be immune to death. This bothered Lord Yama, the god of death, who prayed to Lord Shiva to correct this so the balance of the universe could be maintained. Lord Shiva answered his prayers and gave him a seat, too, on the pedestal. And thus, the temple came to have two Lingas – one dedicated to Lord Yama, the god of death, and the other to Lord Shiva in his Eshwara or life-giving form. Put together, the divine site was considered the sacred home of the god known as Kaleshwara, the god who could give life and take it and liberate people from the constant cycle of birth and death.

Many years after these ancient Shiva temples were built, legend speaks of a wall built by Vishnu that connected these three temples together to fortify the sacred land they were built on. Vishnu built the wall to protect the people from a giant called Nishambhu. Having kept the people safe, Vishnu battled the giant for many years along with all the gods and goddesses who fought on his side. Finally, after having vanquished the giant, Vishnu, too, settled down on the banks of a river that flowed near these three temples. He is said to have called the land he lived on Trilangam.

What do these stories have to do with Telengana, you might ask? Well, much like the name that Vishnu gave to the land, in ancient times the land connected by the presence of the three ancient Shiva temples was called Trilingadesham, or the land of three lingas – Draksharamam, Srisailam, and Kaleeshwaram. Trilingadesham was also known as Trilinga, Telunga, or Telugu. The language of this land was also known as Telugu. Over time, the word Trilinga also changed to Tilinga, and then to Tilingani, and finally Telengana. This is how Telengana came to be the name of the land of this state and how it also came to denote the people who spoke the Telugu language.

KNOW YOUR STATES

- Telangana, formerly a part of Andhra Pradesh, became a state in 2014, making it India's youngest state. The language spoken in both states is Telugu.
- Hyderabad is the capital of Telangana. Hyderabad is also known as the city of pearls because of the major pearl trade in the city. The growing tech industry here has also led to a nickname – Cyberabad.
- Telangana has beautiful landscapes, including the Nagarjuna Sagar Dam and Kuntala Waterfalls.
- Chindu Bhagavatham is a famous theatre art form from Telangana.
- Telangana is famous for crafts like Bidri craft, Banjara Needle crafts, and Dokra metal crafts.
- Telangana is home to the famous Olympic silver medallist P.V. Sindhu. She is the first and only Indian so far to become the Badminton World Champion. She was the first Indian woman to win two Olympic medals.
- Telangana has many famous historical monuments, like Charminar, Golconda Fort, and the Qutb Shahi tombs.

25

TRIPURA

The Land of King Tripur

As the story goes, the state of Tripura was named after a legendary demon king called Tripurasura. He was so powerful that he was able to vanquish all the neighbouring kings of the region. In the beginning of his reign, Tripurasura, or King Tripur as he was called, was a huge believer of Lord Shiva. He ruled in Shiva's name, urging his subjects to be followers of Shiva as well. Everything was done according to how King Tripur thought Shiva would like it.

The other gods who were watching did not like this one bit. One by one, they all made their way to Tripurasura's kingdom to try their luck and see if anyone would worship them too. But they had no luck. The king and people were determined to follow Shiva. Upset, the gods went to Lord Brahma and asked him to intervene on their behalf.

'Ask the king to worship us too,' they said.

Lord Brahma shook his four heads. 'I will do no such thing,' he said.

'King Tripurasura and his people are doing nothing wrong. They are following all the laws and all the rules. It is up to them to choose which god they would like to worship.'

Miffed at Lord Brahma's refusal, the gods went all the way up to Mount Kailash to meet Lord Shiva.

'Ask the king to worship us too,' they said to Lord Shiva.

'I can't do that, my fellow gods,' Lord Shiva said, 'King Tripurasura and his subjects have the right to decide which god they want to worship and which festivals they want to celebrate. As his chosen god, I will only intervene if he does something wrong. But there has been no wrongdoing on his part, so my hands are tied.'

The disappointed gods went to Lord Vishnu, the preserver, and asked for his help.

He sighed and said exactly what Lord Brahma and Lord Shiva had said. However, he added one more thing that gave the gods hope.

'At the end of the day, dear gods, King Tripurasura is an asura and his subjects are human. They might not be doing anything wrong now, but there might come a time when the king makes a mistake, and he takes a wrong turn. At that point, the gods might be able to step in and make a difference.'

Just as Lord Vishnu had predicted, within a few years, a change came over King Tripurasura. A man called Mundi came into town and somehow caught the eye of the king. He steered the king away from good deeds, education, and knowledge. King Tripurasura who was once known for compassion and justice fell into bad ways. Chaos erupted in his kingdom. His subjects were terrified at the way things had changed. They were banned from learning new subjects. People were executed for the smallest things. Oppression was widespread. People, whether they be man, woman, or child, old or young, were too scared to walk on the streets.

The king had changed so completely after his time with Mundi that he became arrogant, heartless, proud, and merciless. He no longer worshipped Lord Shiva, nor did he have time to study the ancient scriptures or reflect on how to be a just and noble ruler for his people.

The gods who had been waiting for a time just like this one, rushed back up Mount Kailash and took the news to Lord Shiva.

'See, Lord Shiva, see what has happened to King Tripurasura. See how he mistreats his subjects and neglects his kingdom. Surely, you can punish him now,' the gods said to Lord Shiva.

Lord Shiva could not believe what he was hearing. He closed all his eyes and sent the gaze of his third eye to King Tripurasura's kingdom. He was shocked to see the reality there. Once a land where every subject felt equal in the eyes of the king and the law, was now a land where poverty existed in high numbers. No one had time to think about being a good person and being compassionate. Shiva knew he had to go down and rid this once excellent land and restore it to its past greatness.

Shiva made his way to the court of King Tripurasura and revealed himself in all his glory. There would have been a time when King Tripurasura would have been happy beyond all imagination to see his beloved Lord Shiva in front of him. But the Tripurasura standing in front of Shiva did not even greet the god. Shiva's heart filled with sadness. He raised his trident, his *trishul*, and aimed it at King Tripurasura's heart. Shiva knew that once it touched Tripurasura's heart it would destroy all that was bad within him – all the arrogance, all the pride would instantly evaporate, cleansing his heart and bringing back the kind and wonderful King Tripurasura that had once captured the hearts of all his subjects. But the trishul was so powerful that the king would not be able to withstand its power. His soul would rise to heaven cleansed of all its sins and all that would remain would be the memories of what a good man he had once been.

Blessing the land and King Tripurasura's family, Shiva let the trishul fly. The divine weapon found its mark, and all the evil in the land ceased to exist. The people celebrated the defeat of evil but grieved their king who had once been the best they had ever seen. Lord Shiva held an arm up to silence their cries and told them that not all had been lost. King Tripurasura's Queen Heeravati had been blessed with a baby, a son whom they had named Trilochan. Lord Shiva promised that Trilochan would always have the hand of heaven to guide him as he grew up and took care of the kingdom. And to commemorate the memory of King Tripurasura, the land where he once ruled would be named Tripura and that is still the name that we know it by today.

KNOW YOUR STATES

- The other name for Tripura is Hill Tiperah, which was its name when it was a princely kingdom before joining the Indian Union.
- Agartala is the capital of Tripura. There are many Agarwood trees in the region. So, no surprise that the name Agartala is derived from the word *agar*, a fragrant dark wood, and *tala*, which means 'underneath,' together referring to the wood and the fragrance made from it.
- Besides Bengali and Kokborok (the Tripuri language), many tribal languages are spoken in Tripura, showing its rich cultural diversity.
- Tripura is home to nineteen distinct tribes and many sub-tribes.
- Tripura is also home to twenty-one different species of bamboo.
- Two of the state's largest festivals are Kharchi Puja and Garia Puja.
- Tripura is known for monuments and historical sites like Ujjayanta Palace, Unakoti rock carvings, and Neermahal Water Palace.

26

UTTAR PRADESH

The Land in the North

A long, long time ago a wise king named Manu was meditating along the banks of a mighty river that flowed through the capital city of his kingdom. King Manu had no children and was very old. He often wondered who would take care of the land he had ruled over after he was gone. After he was done meditating, King Manu got up and went to wash his hands in the waters of the fast-flowing river. Suddenly a small fish came into his hands. Manu held it and was just about to release it back into the water, when much to his surprise the fish spoke up.

'O King, please help me. I am a poor helpless fish. There are many creatures bigger than me in these waters ready to prey on me. Please save my life.'

Manu was a compassionate man. He carefully held the fish in his hands and carried it back to the little hut he had on the banks of the river. This is where he had been staying ever since he left his palace. He found a small jar and put the fish into it. Manu took care of the fish and fed it, happy to have a companion. The next day when he woke up, though, the tiny fish had grown so big that the jar was too small for it.

'O King, this is not enough space for me. Could you move me to a bigger body of water?' the fish asked Manu.

Manu scooped the fish out and moved him to a pond that was nearby. However, by the next day, the fish had

grown again. The fish was so big now that it could not even move in the pond Manu had placed it in.

'O King, I have to ask you for your help again. This space is not enough. And now that I am bigger than my predators, it is time for me to go back to the river. Can you help me get back again?' the fish asked Manu.

Even though the fish was now many times bigger than Manu, the king agreed to help the fish. He grabbed it with all his strength and somehow took it all the way to the river he had found the fish in.

Soon enough, the fish had outgrown the river as well and now he requested Manu's help in making his way to the ocean. By now, Manu knew that this was no ordinary fish. But he helped it all the same. The moment the fish touched the ocean, it grew to epic proportions and started gleaming with a divine light.

'You are a good and just human, Manu. As you might have guessed, I am an avatar of Lord Vishnu. I have been born on earth to help you protect mankind. In seven days, the world as you know it will end because everything will be submerged in a flood. I need you to make a huge boat and collect seven of the world's wisest people, the seeds of all the plants, and an animal each from all the animals that you know. I will appear then and lead your boat away to safety,' the fish declared.

Manu bowed down to the giant fish and rushed away to do his bidding. In seven days, he returned having completed all the tasks that the fish had asked him to do. The fish was waiting for him with a giant tusk now growing upwards from his head. Manu fastened the boat onto the horn and the fish took care of the rest. The fish swam out into the open waters of the ocean, where the boat rose and fell along with the swelling waves. Onward it went till it reached the peaks on the northern mountains. There the fish kept Manu and all the living beings on the boat in safety till the flood waters receded. Once the floods had cleared away, the fish called for Manu.

'Oh King, as you once saved me, it is now your turn to save the rest of humanity. Go forth and begin the next era of time.'

With the fish's wise words ringing in his ears, Manu decided to establish a kingdom that would be home to leaders who would always do the right thing no matter what challenges were ahead of them. King Manu was the only human left. How would he find people who could continue to be fair and just rulers after him? Up in the heavens, Brahma was watching Manu. He smiled and shook his head, making Manu sneeze. And out of King Manu's right nostril jumped a young man called

Ikshavaku who would go on to establish a kingdom that would be known for its rulers.

The name of Ikshavaku's kingdom was Kosala, bordered by the Gomti River in the west and the Sarpika River in the south. Ikshavaku went on to establish the Suryavansha dynasty that would go on to have famous kings and queens. Kosala grew in fame and was known all around the land. In time, it became the kingdom of Prince Rama, the son of Dasharatha, with its capital at Ayodhya. Legend says that after Rama gave his throne to his two sons, Lava and Kusha, Kosala became known by two names – Uttara Kosala and Dakshina Kosala, where *uttara* meant 'north' and *dakshina* meant 'south.' Uttara Kosala welcomed people of all faiths and beliefs, which is probably why it was a land where Gautama Buddha, the founder of Buddhism, and Mahavira, one of the most important teachers of Jainism visited often.

As time passed, due to mergers with other kingdoms and other events, the name Kosala disappeared into the mists of time. People of the land continued to refer to it as the Northern Region though, which translated to Hindi as Uttar Pradesh. And that is how the state named Uttar Pradesh got its name.

KNOW YOUR STATES

- Uttar Pradesh is known as the Sugar Bowl of India. Uttar Pradesh ranks highest among the Indian states in the production of sugarcane.
- Lucknow is the capital of Uttar Pradesh. There are many stories about how Lucknow got its name. One says that the city was named after a famous architect, Lakhna Ahir, who made the fort Qila Lakhan. Some say it was named after Lakshman, the younger brother of Lord Ram from the Ramayana. According to the second story, the town was first called Lakshmanpura, then Lakhanpur, and later Lucknow.
- The state animal of Uttar Pradesh is the Barasingha or the swamp deer.
- Uttar Pradesh is the site of the world's largest gathering of people – the Kumbh Mela.
- It is home to the iconic Taj Mahal. The Taj Mahal was built by the Mughal Emperor Shah Jahan in memory of his wife, Mumtaz Mahal.

27

UTTARAKHAND

The Land Protected by the Mahasu Brothers

The land that we now know as Uttarakhand was once known as Devabhoomi or the land of the gods. People believe this land has always been home to gods and goddesses and mystical mountain beings known as *devatas*. This was where the river goddess Ganga first stepped onto earth, becoming the only river that flows through heaven, earth, and the underworld.

It is even believed that the Pandavas from the Mahabharata also stayed here for a while. Anyone who is familiar with the epic knows of the time that the Pandavas were in exile. The five brothers – Yudhishthira, Bhima, Arjuna, Nakula, and Sahadeva – and their wife, Draupadi, were said to have lived in this northern land, safely hidden from prying eyes. Draupadi fell in love with the lush natural beauty of the land – surrounded by flowers of all kinds. And far in the distance were the northern mountains soaring up to touch heaven. It is said that the Pandavas lived here for nine days and they asked the architect of the gods, Vishwakarma, to build them a temple here. The place where the Pandavas lived is said to be Hanol. There are huge stones that are said to have been used by Bhima, the strongest Pandava, to do his daily exercise. The people of Hanol still believe that only one with the purest of heart will ever be able to lift these stones.

Hanol is a tiny village high up in the mountains, nestled along a stream, and bordered by lush pine forests. Many, many years ago the people of Hanol were bothered by demons who wandered not only through the village but also through the rest of Uttarakhand, devouring people and devastating the land. The fiercest demon of all was Kirmir. Kirmir enjoyed hurting people, and he also enjoyed eating them. He had eaten all seven sons of a villager named Huna Bhatt. But Kirmir wasn't done yet. After gobbling the sons, he growled that he would eat Huna Bhatt's wife next.

Devastated at the loss of their sons and terrified by what was to come, the pair prayed to all the gods they could think of for protection. One night, a mountain goddess named Hatkeshwari Devi appeared in their dreams and told them that their life was about to change. Four devata brothers would soon emerge from the mountains, strengthened by the pure air and the fragrance of the many flowers, and blessed by the waters of the Ganga and the Tons River; these brothers would decimate the demons who had plagued the people of this northern land.

The goddess directed Huna Bhatt to first get a plough made of pure silver and shoes made of pure gold. He was also asked to collect a pair of bullocks that had never been attached to a yoke before. Then Huna Bhatt was asked to plough his fields on the seventh day of every week, while wearing the shoes and having yoked the bullocks to the silver plough. Huna Bhatt

did what the goddess asked him to do week after week. Meanwhile, the demons kept wreaking havoc across the land.

Finally, as Huna Bhatt ploughed the field on the seventh day of the week, for the sixth time, the four devata brothers emerged. Their names were Vasik, Boutha, Pavasi, and Chalda. And together they were known as the Mahasu brothers. Each of the four brothers were accompanied by an attendant known as a *bir*. The Mahasu brothers instructed Huna Bhatt to plough the field one more time. And on the seventh furrow, out came their heavenly mother, Devlaadli Devi. Devlaadli Devi raised her hand and an army of warriors emerged from the fields like mushrooms.

'We who have emerged from these northern lands will protect the northern lands and everyone who lives here,' the goddess thundered.

The army under the leadership of the brothers immediately got to work, fighting the demons. One by one the demons were vanquished. All that remained was the leader, Kirmir. One of the brothers, Chalda devata, immediately made his way to a mountain called Mount Khanda, where the demon Kirmir was said to be hiding out in a ravine. Chalda devata met the demon in a fierce battle. They fought so hard that people believe you can still see the marks of the devata's sword on the rocks up there. Finally, Kirmir fell as well, and the Mahasu brothers were lauded as the guardians of this northern land.

After the battle, the brothers decided to divide the land into different parts so that they could protect it from any evil that might try and attack it. The brother named Pavasi, settled down at a place called Thadiyar. The brother named Boutha was wounded during the war and ended up with a permanent limp. As he could not walk too far, he was allowed to take over the village of Hanol, where they had emerged from. Vasik was given the land of Maindranath. This left Chaldu Devata, who was the one who had vanquished Kirmir. Chaldu was given the responsibility of being on the move to look after all the lands that fell under the Mahasu brothers' protection.

The Mahasu brothers are still believed to live in and around this northern land, even though they cannot be physically seen anymore. These four devata brothers are considered to be gods of justice and people believe that praying to them will help them arrive at a fair and just decision.

The land of the Mahasu brothers and the Devlaadli Devi and the Ganges and other gods and goddesses continues to be a lush land known for its stunning natural beauty. As you read the story, you must have noticed how we called the region the stories are set in, the 'northern lands.' That is because this is exactly why this state is called Uttarakhand. The word Uttarakhand can be divided into two parts, *Uttara* and *Khand*. Uttara means 'north' and khand means 'land,' giving the state the name that we know it by today.

KNOW YOUR STATES

- Dehradun is the capital city of Uttarakhand. The name Dehradun is derived from the Hindi words *dehra* and *doon*. Dehra is said to mean 'shrine' and doon means 'valley.' The land was originally known as Dehra in reference to a shrine in the region, and later became associated with the word doon, giving birth to the name Dehradoon, which eventually became Dehradun.
- The Chipko Movement began in Uttarakhand. During this movement, villagers, primarily women, hugged trees to stop contractors from cutting them down.
- Two of India's sacred rivers, the Ganga and the Yamuna originate here.
- Uttarakhand is home to Tehri Dam, India's tallest dam.
- The Valley of Flowers National Park in Uttarakhand is a UNESCO World Heritage site.

28

WEST BENGAL

The Land of the Vanga

Many, many years ago there was a kingdom and a king who shared its name. You see, both the king and the kingdom were named Vanga. King Vanga was named in part after a god called Singbonga. Singbonga was a sun god who the people worshipped for light and life. Vanga was the adopted son of King Valli who was the ruler who had established the kingdom of Vanga. King Valli wanted people to think of his son and his kingdom to be as powerful as the sun god. Just as life on earth would cease without the sun, people would need to live in the kingdom of Vanga ruled by King Vanga to lead a happy and fulfilled life.

The kingdom of Vanga was bordered by the sea. So, it was not surprising that the kingdom was known for its excellent navy and control of the seas. Vanga was so famous that it was even mentioned in the Indian epic the Mahabharata. It was said that there were many holy places and sacred water bodies across the kingdom of Vanga. Arjuna was said to have visited all of them over his twelve years of exile. Vanga was well known for its soft cotton fabric. The kingdom also had a strong military with a battalion that was made up of the best war elephants. The people of Vanga were said to be intelligent and well-versed in all things literary. Over the years, the kingdom grew and grew. Kings and queens were crowned the rulers. They completed their reins and then they moved only for the next set of rulers to rise up. This is how we reach the time of King Suratha.

King Suratha of Vanga was a powerful and benevolent ruler. But he was an unlucky man who had treacherous ministers in his court. Due to the scheming and betrayal of these ministers, King Suratha ended up losing a war with terrible consequences. The defeat meant that the king would have to give up the kingdom of Vanga. Having lost his throne, he left his beloved kingdom behind and made his way out into the world to explore his fortune. Having travelled far and wide, King Suratha ended up in the town of Bolipur. Here he met a merchant called Vaishya Samadhi. Like the king, the merchant too was reeling from a bad bout of misfortune. He had come to Bolipur because he had heard of a holy man who could help him find luck and good fortune again. The merchant told King Suratha of the holy man called Medhas Muni. This was the man who would help them both. However, it was not easy to get to Medhas Muni. He lived in his hermitage deep in the woods of the Garh jungle.

'And the jungle is full of wild animals of all kinds, animals that will not be easy to ignore,' the merchant told the king.

'What kind of animals?' the king asked in wonder.

'Tigers, elephants, rhinos, wolves, crocodiles, and the list goes on,' the merchant said.

The king shivered a bit thinking of the dense, dark jungles and the animals that must fill every nook and cranny of it. But he knew that he could not let the wilderness stop him from getting to the one person who might be able to help him. King Suratha knew that he had to get his kingdom back no matter what obstacles and challenges were in his way. So, King Suratha and the merchant set forth to find Medhas Muni. After days of carefully trekking through the jungle, the pair finally found the ashram of the holy man.

The hermitage was sheltered by tall trees, and it stood as a peaceful spot amidst the sounds of the wilderness.

Medhas Muni welcomed both the weary travellers with open arms. He invited the king and the merchant to rest in the lush gardens of the ashram and promised that he would help them find the path to happiness again. As the sage, the king, and the merchant spent time together, Medhas Muni started telling them the story of the battle between Goddess Durga and the demon Mahishasura. He spoke about the goddess's strength, power, and resilience while setting upon the biggest challenge she had ever faced. As King Suratha and Vaishya Samadhi listened to the sage's tales about the goddess, they found themselves filled with awe and inspiration. The sage urged them to believe in the goddess and worship her. And so, King Suratha and the merchant made a clay image of Goddess Durga and prayed. As they chanted the mantras that Medhas Muni had taught them, they felt themselves become courageous again. For three years, King Suratha sat on the banks of the river and meditated on this clay image of Goddess Durga. Finally, she appeared and asked him what he needed.

'O Durga devi, grant me the strength to conquer my enemies and gain my kingdom back,' the king replied.

Goddess Durga held up her hand. 'Go back to your kingdom, King Suratha. Your enemies have been weakened, and you will be able to regain all that you have lost. And I will always be with you whenever you need me,' she said.

Armed with this boon, King Suratha marched back to the kingdom of Vanga. The once treacherous ministers of his court were alarmed to see the king back in all his power. It was just as the Goddess had promised. Her invisible presence was with him every step of the way. The ministers bowed down to King Suratha and promised that they would never betray him again. King Suratha was able to take back his kingdom. Ever since then, the kingdom of Vanga has always celebrated Goddess Durga with a festival that lasts for nine days.

As time passed, the kingdom of Vanga came to be known as Bang, Banga, and later Banglah. Bangla also became the name of the language that was spoken in the kingdom.

As speakers of Bangla migrated to other lands, the land that was originally known as the kingdom of Vanga came to be known as Paschim Banga. *Paschim* translates to 'west' in English and *banga* translates to 'Bengal,' giving us the name of the state that we know as West Bengal.

KNOW YOUR STATES

- Kolkata, formerly known as Calcutta, is the capital of West Bengal. Kolkata was also the capital of India during the British rule before it was moved to New Delhi in 1911.
- Kolkata gets its name from Kalighat, the ground of Goddess Kali. Kolkata is also known as the city of joy for its vibrant festivals.
- Bengali, or Bangla, is the main language spoken in West Bengal.
- The National Library of India in Kolkata is the nation's largest public library. Originally established as Calcutta Public Library in 1836, it has over 2.2 million books, ancient manuscripts, and journals.
- West Bengal is home to the Great Banyan Tree, one of the world's oldest banyan trees, believed to be over 250 years old.
- The Sundarbans in West Bengal is a UNESCO World Heritage site known for its unique ecosystem and as the home of the famous Bengal tiger.

29

THE UNION TERRITORIES

In addition to its many states, India has eight Union Territories*. Unlike states, which have their own governments, Union Territories are smaller regions directly governed by the Central Government of India. Each Union Territory has its own unique features and importance.

These Union Territories are:

1. Andaman and Nicobar Islands
2. Chandigarh
3. Dadra and Nagar Haveli and Daman and Diu
4. Delhi
5. Jammu and Kashmir
6. Ladakh
7. Lakshadweep
8. Puducherry

* This information as per 2025

Andaman and Nicobar Islands

Andaman and Nicobar Islands became a Union Territory of India in 1956, with Port Blair as its capital. There are many stories behind the names of these islands. According to Italian travellers from the fifteenth century, the name Andaman meant 'island of gold.' Another story goes that Hanuman, the iconic monkey god from the Ramayana, stopped here on his way to Lanka. The name Andaman is said to be a local pronunciation of Hanuman that then ended up becoming the name of the island. The Andaman Islands are home to the world's most isolated tribe, the Sentinelese. The Sentinelese are said to be the last uncontacted indigenous people in the world.

The name Nicobar is said to have been derived from the Tamil words *nakkam* and *varam*. *Nakkam* means 'naked' and *varam* means 'land.' Put together, *Nakkamvaram* was said to have meant 'a desolate coastline' or 'an island where the indigenous tribes did not wear clothes.' These islands are often referred to in old historical documents as Nakkavaram. As time passed, the Nakkavaram islands came to be called Nicobar Islands.

Chandigarh

Chandigarh became a Union Territory in 1966. This region also functions as the state capital of Punjab and Haryana. You must have already read the stories behind the names of Punjab and Haryana. So here is the story behind the name Chandigarh. The name of this Union Territory comes from the two words *chandi* and *garh*. The word *chandi* is another name for Goddess Durga. The word *garh* means 'house.' Put together, the words mean the house of Goddess Durga, which many believe comes from an ancient temple of the goddess here. Locals believe that this temple was built by the Pandavas during the time of the Mahabharata. It was dedicated to the goddess of power, Chandi. It was because of the presence of this temple that the city came to be known as Chandigarh.

Dadra and Nagar Haveli and Daman and Diu

This lush and beautiful Union Territory is wedged between the states of Maharashtra and Gujarat. This region is home to various indigenous tribes. The most important among these are the Warlis, the Dhodias, and the Koknas. The Dhodia clan came from a place called Dhulia; they were the first people to set foot in this land. As time passed, the name Dadar was born, as if to mean the place where the Dhodia stay.

The name Nagar Haveli comes from the words *nagar* and *haveli. Nagar* comes from the Hindi word for 'city,' and *haveli* is the Hindi word for 'mansion.' You can find the same words in other Indian languages as well. Hence Nagar Haveli literally means 'the city of mansions.'

Daman was named after the Daman Ganga River that flows through western India. This brings us to the final region in this Union Territory – Diu. Diu is an island, and that is where its name comes from as well. The word *diu* is derived from the Sanskrit word *dwipa*, which means 'island.' Over the years, dwipa just slowly became the word Diu in the local language, finally becoming the name of the land.

Delhi

All of us know of New Delhi as the capital of India. New Delhi is a region within Delhi; a Union Territory created in 1956. The land of Delhi has always had a rich and complex history. Many a kingdom and ruler have flourished on this land. Legend says that Delhi was originally known as Indraprastha, the capital of the Pandavas from the epic Mahabharata. Delhi has had many different names since then, but most historians and locals agree that it is also widely known as Dilli. This name is believed to come from a king called Raja Dhillu. Raja Dhillu was one of the first kings to establish a township in this land. The capital city of Raja Dhillu's kingdom was named Dhillika. As time passed, Dhillika was shortened to Dhilli, and eventually to present-day Delhi.

Jammu and Kashmir

The region of Jammu and Kashmir became a Union Territory in 2019. The area was also split into two parts: Jammu and Kashmir, which still has its own local government, and Ladakh, which is managed by the central government. Jammu is said to be named after a legendary king called Jambu Lochan. The local lore has it that many years before Jammu was known by this name, King Jambu Lochan crossed the Tawi River while busy on a hunt. To his astonishment, he saw a deer and a tiger drinking water from the same part of the river. The wise men and ministers who had accompanied him on the hunt explained that this meant that this land was so sacred that no creature who lived here could ever bear a grudge against another. King Jambu Lochan immediately decided to build a capital city here, which he named Jambupura after himself. As time passed, Jambupura came to be known as Jammu.

Kashmir has many fascinating stories about how it got its name. The one thing that is common in all the stories is that Kashmir emerged from under a heavenly lake. According to a twelfth-century book called *Rajatarangini*, the land we call Kashmir was once submerged under a huge lake. However, a holy sage called Kashyapa drained it to make it habitable for humans. The land created by Kashyapa came to be called Kashmir. In Kashmiri, the language of the region, the land is called Kasheer. According to local legends, the lake was drained by two magical beings or djinns called Kashf and Mir. When you put the names together you get Kashfmir that became Kashmir with the passage of time.

Ladakh

Ladakh became a Union Territory in 2019. It is the largest Union Territory at the moment, but it is also one of the least populated. Ladakh has had many names over its long history. It was called Maryul or lowlands by some, even though it is high up in the

Himalayas. It was called Khapa Chan by the local people, which means 'land of snow.' Various ancient Chinese travellers called it by different names too. However, in Tibetan, the local language spoken in the land, it was called Ladvags, meaning 'the land of high passes.' *La* meaning 'land' and *dvags* meaning 'high passes.' The word dvags is pronounced as 'daak' in the language, making the word ladvags sound like la-daak. And this is the word that ended up becoming the name of the land, Ladakh.

Lakshadweep

Lakshadweep became a Union Territory in 1956. In Malayalam and Sanskrit, the word *Laksham* means 'one hundred thousand,' and the word *dwipa* means 'island.' Put together, the words mean 'one hundred thousand islands.' While the name mentions a hundred thousand islands, in reality, Lakshadweep is only made of thirty-six coral islands and is India's smallest Union Territory.

Puducherry

Puducherry officially became a Union Territory in 1963. Till the year 2006, this territory was known as Pondicherry. However, it was rightfully renamed

Puducherry to reflect the original Tamil name of this land. The land known as Puducherry was under French control for a long time. Many, many years ago, before colonialism and long before India as we know it existed, this land was supposed to be the abode of learned scholars. In Sanskrit, the word *veda* stands for knowledge. So, this land was known as Vedapuri. As any place with learned scholars and highly knowledgeable people, this land, too, prospered and people from far-off kingdoms came to hear of it. Traders and travellers came by, and the town started looking different. People started calling it Podikai or Pudivai, which meant 'new village' or 'meeting place.' Podikai or Poduke, as the Roman traders called it, was controlled by many different kingdoms till it ultimately fell into the hands of French colonialists. They created a new settlement there that was called Puducheri in Tamil by the local people. *Pudu* means 'new', and *cheri* means 'town or settlement.' The French interpretation of this word was Pondicherry, and this is what the region was called till 2006, when it was renamed Puducherry in honour of its history.

30

WHY IS INDIA ALSO CALLED BHARAT?

Once upon a time, before the stories of all the states of India, and long before all the Union Territories were carved out, there lived a king who was so powerful that an entire country ended up sharing his name. This is the story of Emperor Bharata.

Emperor Bharata's story starts at the hermitage of Sage Kanva, a long time before Bharata was even born. According to legend, King Dushyanta was hunting in the forests when he came across Sage Kanva's hermitage. Here, Dushyanta met Kanva's adoptive daughter Shakuntala, who turned out to be the most beautiful woman that Dushyanta had ever seen.

In the absence of the sage, the king and Shakuntala became friends and then ended up falling in love. They got married and King Dushyanta promised that the son that would be born to them would be crowned the next king. In time, Shakuntala had a baby who was born with the sign of a *chakra*, or a wheel, on his right hand. On seeing the sign, the baby's grandfather, Sage Kanva, declared that the baby would become a *chakravarti*. The word chakravarti in Sanskrit means 'emperor' in English. Shakuntala's baby was already showing signs of greatness. The story goes that he was born with the strength of ten thousand elephants. Even as a child, the boy was able to subdue the wild beasts of the forest.

King Dushyanta named his son Bharata. According to the Mahabharata, Bharata eventually became king and ended up conquering the world. It is said that Emperor Bharata ruled for twenty-seven thousand years. The kingdom that he inherited and then grew far beyond its original borders came to be known as Bharatavarsha, or the land of Bharata. In time, the land came to be called Bharat. The Constitution of India recognizes both names, with Article 1 stating, 'India, that is Bharat, shall be a Union of States.' This way it acknowledges both the modern name 'India' and the ancient name 'Bharat.'

ACKNOWLEDGEMENTS

Thank you to my parents and grandparents for instilling a deep love of mythology and history in me. Thank you for bequeathing me a treasure trove of legends and lore as my legacy.

Thank you to my children for being my sounding boards and beta readers. I now entrust you with these stories as your legacy.

Thank you to Sagar for taking the kids out of my hair as I rushed to meet deadlines and coaxed stories

out of sources that had been long lost to time. Thank you for making dinner every night and letting me lose myself in my world of words.

I want to thank my entire publishing team at Hachette India for trusting me with telling these stories.

And finally, if you picked up this book because you have heard my stories on my podcast, *Storytelling with Shweta*, or if you have read any of my other books, a huge note of gratitude to you!